Evil: A Guide for the Perplexed

Evil: A Guide for the Perplexed

CHAD MEISTER

continuum

The Continuum International Publishing Group Inc

The Tower Building   80 Maiden Lane,
11 York Road,   Suite 704,
London   New York,
SE1 7NX   NY 10038

www.continuumbooks.com

ISBN: HB:978-1-4411-2089-2 (hardcover)
ISBN: 978-1-4411-2171-4 (paperback)

Library of Congress Cataloging-in-Publication Data
A catalog record for this title is available from the Library of Congress.

Typeset by Deanta Global Publishing Services, Chennai, India
Printed and bound in the United States of America

CONTENTS

PREFACE

There are few topics in the history of Western thought about which more has been published than evil. Works on evil go back as far in intellectual history as publications go. In plays, novels, movies, even art – wherever there is human life and inspiration – we find reflections on and depictions of evil. Evil is ubiquitous.

This book emerged out of much reflection on the origin and nature of evil. I have struggled with this subject on an intellectual level for years. Though I have thought much about evil (probably too much) and done a fair amount of work on the topic, I wonder if a better subtitle for this book might be *A Guide by the Perplexed*! Evil is a subject that no one can fully master, which is probably a good thing. It is simply too large and complex (and dark) a matter. There is much about evil that could not be covered in a single volume like this one, but I do hope that the musings offered here will be a helpful guide through the various issues that arise given the evil that exists in our world. This is a philosophical work on evil, not a historical or psychological or sociological one (though all these areas are significant). If you finish it thinking even a little more clearly about evil, or better yet, come away ready to tackle evil – both intellectually and practically – I will consider this project a good success.

I have learned much from colleagues and friends who have worked on this subject, reading their articles and books, discussing and debating the issues at conferences and in private conversation and brainstorming about future projects related to it. I would especially like to thank Charles Taliaferro, my dialectical comrade in evil. His brilliance on this and many other matters is challenging and inspiring. James Stump has been an invaluable friend and sparring partner on the subject as well, engaging with me in countless 'evil' conversations. I am most appreciative of his astuteness and sagacity. I am indebted to my wife Tammi for the insights she offered throughout the project and, more importantly, for demonstrating how much value there is in the world, despite its evil. Much appreciation goes to Haaris Naqvi, Senior Editor at Continuum Publishing, for his encouragement, guidance, and seeing this project through to the end. I am also grateful to the following people for their wisdom and helpful reflections on the subject: Marilyn McCord Adams, Paul Draper, William Hasker, John Hick, Paul Moser, Michael Murray, Michael Peterson, Michael Rea, William Rowe, Eleonore Stump, Richard Swinburne, Jerry Walls, and Keith Ward. May their tribes increase.

I dedicate this book to my sons, Justin and Joshua. They are goods in my life beyond description and limit and have taught me much about value, love, and the significance of will and choice in a world where evil is an ever-present reality. My wish is that through the challenges they face they will continue to grow and mature into persons of deep character, extraordinary wisdom and striking moral acuity.

CHAPTER ONE

What is evil?

Our world is plagued by evil. Evil is no less real, no less menacing, and no less ubiquitous today than it has ever been. We are faced with evil in all its pernicious forms each and every day as we watch the news, read the newspaper, or simply live out our lives. Yes, evil is always before us. But why? Why is there evil in the world, and why is there so much of it? How did it arise, and how can we respond to it? Before exploring the *whys* and *hows*, we need to first get clear what we are talking about when we use the term 'evil'.

What is evil, exactly? What is its nature? Evil is not easy to precisely define. We use the word in such divergent ways that we wonder if there is truly a singular meaning that captures each and every example of its usage. We might say, for example, that Charles Manson was an evil man, that the local dump gives off an evil smell, that the earthquake in Haiti was an evil event, and that hell is an evil place. But what is the common meaning of evil in each of these examples? Dictionaries offer little help by telling us, for example, that evil is 'the opposite of good' or 'that which is morally reprehensible'. Here, as in many other instances of definition, the meanings of the term are multifarious and often fall short of capturing the depth and complexities of the term they are attempting to define. (A similar problem exists with the word 'love', for we might love our cat, love taking naps, love making love, love spaghetti, love our job, and love our spouse, our friend and our God. What common meaning of love can we find in these examples?) However, just as we find it difficult to offer a universal definition of some terms, we can still know what we are talking about when we use them in different contexts. Evil, oftentimes at least, is like that.

The notion of evil comprises a wide expanse, covering everything harmful and destructive in the world. There are different kinds of evil, so before exploring the various theoretical problems that arise from evil, it will be beneficial to sketch out the terrain when using this enigmatic term. As mentioned above it is difficult, if not downright impossible, to provide a clear and concise definition. Theologians often define evil in terms of sin or transgression against God. Most forms of Hinduism and Buddhism have no creator God, so they don't have the same meaning for evil (nor the same problems) that most theists do, though, as we will see in Chapter 6, they do have issues that need to be addressed given evil and suffering. Daoism, too, has no creator. For Daoists, evil does not exist in itself but is a disharmony in nature or disruption in the balance of things that causes suffering. In many Native American traditions, evil is what reduces our happiness. Philosophers, too, have attempted to define evil in a variety of ways, including that it is a deviation from the proper order of goodness. Even insurance companies chime in and speak of evil in terms of 'acts of God' or, more recently, 'acts of nature'. The meanings and usages of the term are endless.

Rather than attempt a definition of evil, for our purposes it will probably be more fruitful to avoid such an endeavour and move forward with a general sense of the term that we can hopefully agree on. Philosopher David Hume provided a useful list that will, I think, give us this general sense I'm after: 'Were a stranger to drop on a sudden into this world, I would show him, as a specimen of its ills [that is, its evils], a hospital full of disease, a prison crowded with malefactors and debtors, a field of battle strewed with carcasses, a fleet foundering in the ocean, a nation languishing under tyranny, famine, or pestilence.'[1] The list of evils is endless, and it includes such broad notions as *pain* (understood as a physical state where we wish our circumstances were otherwise), *suffering* (understood as a mental state where we wish our circumstances were otherwise), and *injustice* (understood as unfairness, the violation of the rights of others, and uncorrected abuse, neglect or malfeasance). As these terms are often used synonymously with evil in the literature and in common English parlance, so too they will be intermingled throughout this book. Beyond definitions and lists, there are also classifications of evil.

Classifying evil

A standard classification of evil divides it into two broad types: moral and natural. Some examples may help to distinguish them. One of the worst nightmares a parent could experience occurred in Orange County, California, on 10 June 1991. An 11-year-old girl, Jaycee Dugard, was on her way to school when she was abducted at the bus stop. Her stepfather was in eyesight of the event, spotting someone grabbing the girl and shoving her into a pickup truck. The stepfather grabbed his bike and began a frantic chase after them, but to no avail. His stepdaughter was gone in a flash. The horror! Sadly, both the little girl's stepfather and her biological father were suspects in the case early on – as if the tragic event itself wasn't bad enough. Eighteen years later, on 4 August 2009, the dreadful facts finally emerged. Jaycee had been abducted by Phillip Garrido, a rapist and chronic drug abuser, along with his wife, Nancy Garrido, and she had been held captive for 18 years in a concealed area behind their house. During those years Jaycee experienced rape and psychological abuse by Phillip, and she birthed two children by him. Jaycee was finally rescued, almost two decades after her abduction. Evils of this kind are dubbed *moral evils* because they are in some sense the result of a person who is morally blameworthy of the resultant evil. There was intention behind the event, and a person's free will was involved. Some moral evils are of great intensity, as is this horror of child abuse. Other examples include genocide, torture and other terrors inflicted on humans by humans. There are also less severe types of moral evils such as stealing or speaking negatively about someone. In addition, certain defects in one's character are also classified as moral evil, including greed, gluttony, vanity and dishonesty.

Another category of evil has to do not with moral agents, but with naturally occurring events or disasters. Examples of *natural evils* include floods, hurricanes, tornadoes, earthquakes, famine, illness such as leukaemia and Alzheimer's disease, disabilities such as deafness and blindness, and other terrible events which do harm to humans and other living creatures but for which no personal agent is responsible. Consider the earthquake that happened in Haiti on 12 January 2010. The epicentre of the quake occurred approximately 16 miles west of Port-au-Prince, Haiti's capital. The magnitude was a catastrophic 7.0 on the Richter scale and included dozens of powerful aftershocks. It affected roughly three million people, destroying homes, commercial buildings, prisons and sewer systems and killing close to 300,000 people and leaving over a million homeless. Even with countries and individuals around the world providing aid and support, recovery efforts have still hardly scratched the surface.

In Standard English we commonly use the word 'evil' to denote some horrific moral evil of one sort or another. We don't often use it to refer to something that was 'merely' bad, such as lying, or to some naturally occurring event, such as a tornado. But for our purposes in this book it will be used to include all the sorts of 'evil' described above. Two other classifications of evil will also be distinguished in later chapters: gratuitous evil and horrendous evil.

It is not immediately obvious why, if God exists, evil would exist. In order to understand this problem raised by evil, it is important to elucidate what is meant by 'God' within the traditional usage of the term.

Traditional theism and evil

For the Abrahamic faiths – Judaism, Christianity and Islam – God is generally understood as a being who is personal (a being who possesses both mind and will), ultimate reality (the source and ground of all other things), separate from the world yet actively involved in the world (creator and sustainer), and worthy of worship (wholly good, having inherent moral perfection, and excelling in power). The Jewish prophets exalted God throughout their writings: 'Give thanks to the Lord, for he is good; his love endures forever' (Psalm 107.1). Writers of the Christian New Testament also proclaimed the goodness of God as the creator of every good thing: 'Every good and perfect gift is from above, coming down from the Father of the heavenly lights, who does not change like shifting shadows' (James 1.17). And the Qur'an, the holy book of Islam, offers similar depictions of God: 'He is the One God; the Creator, the Initiator, the Designer. To Him belong the most beautiful names. Glorifying Him is everything in the heavens and the earth. He is the Almighty, Most Wise' (Surah 59.24).

The traditional theistic concept of God includes a cluster of properties attributed to God, including the following, which are especially relevant to the problem of evil:

Creator and sustainer of the world

God brought the universe – time, space, matter and energy – into existence and God also sustains the world in existence through time. No created thing can exist at any point in time unless it is held in existence by God. All energies, or causal powers, come from God as well, so nothing could act without being supplied each moment by the energies of God.

Omnipotent

Another property traditionally attributed to God is omnipotence, which is the property of being perfect in power. What does it mean to be perfect in power? Philosophers and theologians have struggled with this question, including the great Christian theologian/ philosopher Thomas Aquinas: '[Even though] all confess that God is omnipotent ... it seems difficult to explain in what His omnipotence precisely consists.'[2] One common meaning of omnipotence is being all powerful; an omnipotent being is capable of doing anything.

Omniscient

The meaning of omniscience has been widely debated, but one prominent historical view is that an omniscient being is completely perfect in knowledge. God knows everything that is a proper object of knowledge, and since only true propositions are proper objects of knowledge (only true propositions can be known), God knows all true propositions. Thus, God's knowledge includes all events – past, present and future.

Omnibenevolent

This is the property of being perfect in benevolence or goodness. The word is also understood to mean being perfectly just, all-loving, wholly merciful, and other similar qualities, depending on how the term 'good' is used. For the Abrahamic faiths, this is an essential attribute of God, and some theologians and philosophers have argued that it is the *central* attribute of God. Each one of the above properties, and perhaps most especially this one, is problematic given the existence of evil.

This difficulty is commonly referred to as *the problem of evil*. However, this problem has taken many forms, so it is probably better to speak of *problems of evil*, as there are various difficulties we are confronted with given evil's reality. In the next chapter, we will tackle some of these problems, but the central problem can be put this way: if the God of traditional theism exists, then no evil should exist; but evil does exist – so the God of traditional theism does not exist.

The problem is that there appears to be an inconsistency between God's nature and the existence of evil. As the ancient Greek philosopher Epicurus (341–270 BCE) concisely put it: 'either God wants to abolish evil, and cannot; or he can, but does not want to. If he wants to, but cannot, he is impotent. If he can, but does not want to, he is wicked. If God can abolish evil, and God really wants to do it, why is there evil in the world?'[3]

In the next chapter, we will investigate ways of trying to make sense of traditional theism given the reality of evil. But other non-traditional approaches have also been made.

Non-traditional accounts of God and evil

There are a number of ways to attempt to explain the problems raised by evil outside the paradigm of traditional theism. Let's hone in on four.

1. God does not exist

One way to deal with problems raised by evil and theism is to simply reject theism altogether. If there is no God, we do not have an issue about why God would allow evil to exist. Problem solved. Or is it? We will explore atheism and evil in Chapter 5. Other forms of non-theism include Buddhism and Hinduism, and we will tackle them in Chapter 6. As we will see, there are still problems of evil that non-theistic approaches need to address, but the real rub seems to be the apparent inconsistency of the existence of evil and an omnipotent, omniscient and omnibenevolent creator God.

2. God exists but is not omnipotent

As we saw above, two of the properties traditionally attributed to God are omnipotence and omniscience. And as noted, a common understanding of divine omnipotence is that God can do anything whatsoever: God can create a world; God can answer prayer; God can do miracles; God can do whatever God wants. But this creates an obvious problem. If God can do anything, then God can abolish evil. But evil is not abolished, it continues on as it always has. Why? Traditional theists have this problem to deal with. But perhaps God is not omnipotent after all. In that case, maybe while God wants to eliminate evil, he cannot.

So is God omnipotent? Can God really do anything whatsoever? Can God create square circles and married bachelors? Can God both exist and not exist simultaneously? What about sinning – can God sin? A few philosophers have thought that absolutely nothing can limit God's power. René Descartes (1596–1650), for example, maintained that God is not limited by anything, including the laws of logic and mathematics. For Descartes, God could make it true that some object P both exists and does not exist at the same time, or that 2 plus 2 equals 5, or that A is identical to the opposite of A.

Most philosophers have not agreed with Descartes on this point, even those who affirm that God is omnipotent. Most have qualified the claim 'God can do anything whatsoever' with a nuanced one such as 'God can do anything that is logically possible' or 'God possesses every power which is logically possible to possess.'[4] Logical possibility means that it does not violate the basic laws of logic, such as the law of non-contradiction (which is that a claim and its opposite cannot both be true). Oxford philosopher Richard Swinburne expounds on this point:

A logically impossible action is not an action. It is what is described by a form of words which purport to describe an action, but do not describe anything which it is coherent to suppose could be done. It is no objection to A's omnipotence that he cannot make a square circle. This is because 'making a square circle' does not describe anything which it is coherent to suppose could be done.[5]

We will see in the next chapter that one of the strongest replies to evil given theism is in agreement with Swinburne's assessment of omnipotence. While defenders of Descartes' view might be unconvinced by rational argumentation against the claim that God is not limited by logic, they certainly could not *argue* the point on rational or logical grounds. To do so would be self-contradictory and incoherent. Furthermore, if God could do the illogical, troubling moral consequences would follow. For example, God could break his promises, or lie, or do anything evil and still be good. Most theists are reticent to affirm that God can perform such immoral, illogical actions.

This view of omnipotence, that God cannot perform certain actions (neither immoral ones nor logically impossible ones), is consistent with the traditional view of omnipotence as meaning *perfect* power rather than *absolute* power. This view would assert that mere power itself is not praiseworthy; only perfect or excellent power is. Since perfect power does not entail breaking promises, or lying, or violating contradictions, God could still be omnipotent and yet be unable to perform them. But the point of the non-traditional account emphasized here is that God is not omnipotent in a more significant way. Perhaps the most outspoken defender of this position is Harold Kushner. In his book *Why Bad Things Happen to Good People* Kushner puts further limits on God. God cannot violate the laws of nature, violate free will, nor violate events which occur by chance. Since evil comes about because of them, God is limited in his ability to deal with evil. While God would like to abolish evil, he simply cannot get the job done – at least not at the current time.

3. God exists but is not omniscient (in the traditional sense)

Just as there are those who challenge the traditional notion of God's omnipotence, there are also those who contest divine omniscience as traditionally understood. In recent times, one set of challenges has arisen from an analysis of the concepts of divine foreknowledge and human free will. If we have free will in a certain sense (libertarian free will, which will be explained later), then the future is open – it is undetermined. There are future events that are neither guaranteed to occur nor precluded from occurring by anything that has already happened. These are called *future contingent events*. For example, if the chance of a sea battle occurring next week is currently neither zero nor one, then it is a future contingent event. It might happen; it might not happen. There is indeterminacy in the world. Some philosophers who believe that there are future contingent events argue that such events cannot be known, even by an 'omniscient' being. So, when God created the world, he did not know exactly how it would unfold. God cannot be held morally culpable for how this world turned out, then, since much of it involved the choices of free persons, undetermined and unknown by God. God did not foreknow the evil that would arise from free individuals, and God did not cause the evil which exists in the world, so God is not responsible for it.

4. God exists but is not all good

The vast majority of theists have historically affirmed the perfection of God. Saint Anselm (1033–1109), a Christian theologian of the medieval period, famously described God this way:

> 'But what art thou, except that which, as the highest of all beings, alone exists through itself, and creates all other things from nothing? For, whatever is not this is less than a thing which can be conceived of. But this cannot be conceived of thee. What good, therefore, does the supreme Good lack, through which every good is? Therefore, thou art just, truthful, blessed, and whatever it is better to be than not to be.'[6]

God is perfect in every attribute, including goodness. Some theists have disagreed. For them, God exists but is not perfectly good. There have not been many theists of this stripe, but there have been some. One Nobel Prize winner who affirmed this view is Elie Wiesel. After suffering in a Nazi concentration camp, he came to the conclusion that God is malicious for allowing events as horrific as the Holocaust. His book *Night* is based on his experiences in Auschwitz and Buchenwald. In it he writes of his own disgust with God and humanity. For Wiesel, everything came to an end during these horrors in the camps: man, history, literature, religion and God. If God is not ultimately good, as Wiesel affirmed, then of course the 'problem of evil' disappears.

5. Evil is not real

One final non-traditional approach to the problem of evil is to deny the reality of evil. As we will see in Chapter 6, certain religious traditions hold the view that evil is unreal, an illusion, and that seen from the right perspective will actually disappear. In Chapter 5, we will discover that some atheist thinkers also hold that objective evil is illusory. If evil is not real, there seems to be no problem of evil.

Before concluding this chapter, something needs to be said about another dimension of evil that is just as important as the intellectual problems most of this book will be focused on. This is what is sometimes called the 'existential problem of evil', for while not an intellectual issue per se, it is a real problem nonetheless.

The existential problem of evil

The existential problem of evil, which has various names including the 'religious problem', 'moral problem', 'pastoral problem', 'psychological problem' or 'emotional problem', is not terribly easy to define or delineate. Perhaps it can be put simply as that existential feel of certain kinds of evil which leads to disbelief in or hatred toward God. Philosopher Alvin Plantinga describes this problem:

> The theist may find [an existential] problem in evil; in the presence of his own suffering or that of someone near to him he may find it difficult to maintain what he takes to be the proper attitude towards God. Faced with great personal suffering or misfortune, he may be tempted to rebel against God, to shake his fist in God's face, or even to give up belief in God altogether.[7]

An example may clarify the meaning and power of the problem. A number of years ago I was standing in line with a group of friends at a restaurant. We were engaged in a theological discussion about the nature of God and evil (I grant that I have unusual friends and we have unusual dinner conversation) when a person in front of us asked if we were talking about God. I answered that we were. She then told us that she quit believing in God about two years ago. While her father was suffering and dying of cancer, she decided that she could no longer believe in God. And if he does exist, she said, she hates him. As she told us her story, her emotions bubbled to the surface. I could almost feel her pain and anguish as tears began to stream down her face in agony over her lost father.

This is a clear case of the existential problem of evil. It's not that this young woman was offering reasoned arguments for her feelings and thoughts about God given pain and suffering (although she may well have had them). Rather, she was expressing the pain she suffered and perhaps even her bitterness toward a God who would allow her father to suffer as he had. In such cases it usually doesn't matter much at the time whether there are intellectual responses to the problems of evil. For persons going through such experiences there is a willful, perhaps even obdurate, and sometimes, I would add, warranted, rejection of God because of experienced evil. In situations such as this, one's emotions are at the fore rather than one's intellect and this state calls for something other than rational engagement.

One theologian expresses it the following way. "Think of a young child who goes out to play on a playground. Sometime during her play, she falls and skins her knee. She runs to her mother for comfort. Now, her mother can do any number of things. She can tell her daughter that this has happened because she was running too fast and not watching where she was going – she must be more careful next time. The mother, if she knew them, might even explain the laws of physics and causation that were operating to make her child's scrape just the size and shape it is. The mother might even expound for a few moments on the lessons *God* is trying to teach her child from this experience. If she then pauses and asks her daughter, 'Do you understand, Sweetheart?', don't be surprised if the little girl replies, 'Yes, Mommy, but it still hurts!' All the explanation at that moment doesn't stop her pain. The child doesn't need a discourse; she needs her mother's hugs and kisses. There will be a time for the discourse later; now she needs comfort".[8]

With respect to the existential problem of evil, it is important to note that the 'problem' here is not really an *argument* at all, and thus is not in need of a logical, rational response. When an individual is personally confronted with significant evil and suffering, the main thing he or she needs is not a logical or theoretical response to evil, but rather care, sympathy and friendship. As Plantinga puts it, in those moments of pain a person needs not 'philosophical enlightenment' but rather 'pastoral care'.[9] But the existential and theoretical problems are not entirely divorced, for existential encounter certainly affects one's theorizing, and one's theories are not entirely disconnected from one's experiences. Both sets of problems are important and need to be considered when discussing problems of evil.

Responding to evil

The reality of evil raises many questions, including those having to do with how best to respond to or eliminate it. These sorts of questions are no doubt some of the most important. They are in the genre of what is sometimes dubbed 'practical problems of evil', and they should – no doubt, they *must* – be the kinds of questions human beings engage with and respond to if we are to foster a world of true peace, harmony, love and goodness. Along these lines, philosopher Grace Jantzen makes the following important point:

> [The problem of evil as traditionally discussed] focuses on God rather than on human agency: why does God permit natural evils? Why does God permit human beings to do evil? Again, whatever the answer to these questions, and whether those evaluating the answers think them adequate or not, the focus of attention is diverted within this presentation away from what human beings are doing or might be doing to inflict or prevent evil, away from the earth and into the transcendent realm ... By refusing to engage with the question of the human distribution of evil ... it is possible to evade questions of domination and victimization while still appearing to 'deal with' the problem of evil.[10]

I certainly do not want to evade the practical dimensions of evil, and in the final chapter we will return to this matter of responding to evil. But the central concern of this book has to do with intellectual problems raised by the reality of evil. These problems are not the moral and pragmatic ones of what should be done to ameliorate or eliminate pain and suffering, as non-trivial as those are. Rather, they are the theoretical problems of making sense of the reality of evil in the world in which we find ourselves, given the worldview we affirm. The plausibility of a religion or worldview to some extent depends upon its capacity for providing a coherent and livable schema for understanding our experiences of evil and good. As we will see throughout the pages ahead, the theoretical problems that arise because of evil confront all persons irrespective of their interpretation of the world, whether religious or non-religious. As we are in a profound sense servile to our beliefs and ideas, exploring the issues that arise because of evil and how they relate to our broader understanding of the world is an important enterprise.

We will examine conceptual problems raised by evil and suffering as they confront various worldviews. But the central theoretical problems of evil, as they have been historically developed in the English-speaking world, are focused on the alleged incompatibility of the coexistence of a good, loving and all-powerful God on the one hand and evil on the other, for it is here that the problems seem most acute. So this is where we will expend much of our energies: exploring the challenges and conundrums raised by these seemingly dissonant beliefs. It is to these theistic challenges that we now turn.

Further reading

Adams, Marilyn M. and Robert M. Adams, eds. 1990. *The Problem of Evil*. New York: Oxford University Press. (A scholarly collection of essays from a variety of perspectives by leading philosophers.)

Feinberg, John S. 2004. *The Many Faces of Evil: Theological Systems and the Problem of Evil*. 3rd ed. Wheaton, IL: Crossway.

Howard-Snyder, Daniel, ed. 1996. *The Evidential Argument from Evil*. Bloomington, IN: Indiana University Press.

Hume, David. 1955. *Dialogues Concerning Natural Religion*, ed. H. D. Aiken. Parts 10 and 11. New York: Hafner Publishing.

Lewis, Clive Staples 1962. *The Problem of Pain*. New York: Macmillan. (Lewis focuses on the value of pain and suffering as God's 'megaphone' to rouse a morally deaf world.)

Mackie, John L. 1982. *The Miracle of Theism*. Oxford: Clarendon Press. (See especially his chapter on the problem of evil.)

Meister, Chad and Charles Taliaferro, general eds. forthcoming. *The History of Evil* in six volumes: *Evil in Antiquity* (vol. 1); *Evil in the Middle Ages* (vol. 2); *Evil in the Early Modern Age* (vol. 3); *Evil in the 18th and 19thCenturies* (vol. 4); *Evil in the Early 20th Century* (vol. 5); *Evil from the Mid-20th Century to Today* (vol. 6). Durham, UK: Acumen Press. (A massive work on the history, scope and nature of evil from a philosophical perspective.)

Peterson, Michael L. 1998. *God and Evil: An Introduction to the Issues*. Boulder, CO: Westview Press. (An excellent general introduction to the topic in print.)

CHAPTER TWO

Problems of evil

We saw in the previous chapter that the reality of evil poses difficulties for the major theistic religions, for they each affirm the existence of a perfectly good, all-knowing and all-powerful deity – one who *could*, and seemingly *should*, eliminate the evil, pain and suffering in the world. Yet evil persists. Why? If God exists, why did God create, and why does God permit, a world with such vast amounts of horror and terror? In this chapter, we will home in on several specific problems of evil as they have been articulated in recent years. These problems have to do with reconciling belief in God with the reality of evil. Like evil itself, the problems are multifaceted.

The logical problem

On one formulation of the problem of evil, what's called the *logical problem*, the conclusion is quite strong: God *cannot* exist. In the mid-twentieth century, this argument was developed most effectively by the atheist philosopher J. L. Mackie, and the central issue is the alleged logical inconsistency of the following two claims:

1 God (an omnipotent, omniscient and omnibenevolent being) exists, and
2 Evil exists.

The meaning of the charge of logical inconsistency should be fairly obvious. Two claims that are contradictory cannot both be true. Consider these two claims:

3 The United Nations was founded in 1945.
4 No international organizations were founded in 1945.

Clearly, 3 and 4 cannot both be true, for they violate the law of non-contraction. On the widely held assumption that contradictory claims are necessarily false, if claims 1 and 2 are in indeed contradictions, at least one of them must be false. If it is true that evil exists (claim 2), and most people believe that it is, claim 1 must be false – God must not exist.

In Chapter 6, we will explore views that do not take it as given that evil actually exists. But for now let's grant this assumption: there really is objective evil in the world. Even so, unlike 3 and 4, it is not immediately clear that claims 1 and 2 *are* logically incompatible. In attempting to demonstrate that they are, Mackie developed an argument which can be delineated this way:

  i. A wholly good being always eliminates evil as far as it can.
  ii. There are no limits to what an omnipotent and omniscient being can do.
  iii. So, if a wholly good, omnipotent and omniscient being exists, it eliminates evil completely (from i and ii).
  iv. Evil has not been eliminated completely.
  v. Thus a wholly good, omnipotent and omniscient being does not exist (from iii and iv).[1]

If this argument is sound (that is, if the premises are true and the conclusion deductively follows from them, which it does), it provides proof that God's existence is impossible – logically impossible. God cannot exist.

This argument is concise and, at first blush, persuasive. So the burden is upon the theist to rebut the charge of logical inconsistency. The most significant rebuttal to date has been offered by the Christian philosopher Alvin Plantinga in what he calls the *free will defense*. In this rebuttal, Plantinga attempts to demonstrate that claims 1 and 2 can both be true – that they are not contradictory after all. He does this by proposing a third claim that is consistent with 1 and which, along with 1, implies 2. The third claim is simply that premise ii (that there are no limits to what an omnipotent and omniscient being can do) *may* be false. It could be that even an omnipotent and omniscient being has certain limitations. Plantinga uses contemporary logic and the notion of possible worlds to make his case (the phrase 'possible worlds' is a semantic device which formalizes the notion of what the world might have been like; a statement is necessarily true, then, if and only if it is true in every possible world):

> A world containing creatures who are significantly free (and freely perform more good than evil actions) is more valuable, all else being equal, than a world containing no free creatures at all. Now God can create free creatures, but He can't *cause* or *determine* them to do only what is right. For if He does so, then they aren't significantly free after all; they do not do what is right *freely*. To create creatures capable of *moral good*, therefore, He must create creatures capable of moral evil; and He can't give these creatures the freedom to perform evil and at the same time prevent them from doing so. As it turned out, sadly enough, some of the free creatures God created went wrong in the exercise of their freedom; this is the source of moral evil. The fact that free creatures sometimes go wrong, however, counts neither against God's omnipotence nor against His goodness; for He could have forestalled the occurrence of moral evil only by removing the possibility of moral good.[2]

So Mackie's logical argument from evil is unsuccessful because it is logically possible (it *may* be the case) that in creating a world with free creatures – a valuable world – God (an omnipotent, omniscient and omnibenevolent being) may be unable to ensure that this world has no evil in it. And it may be the case that God would create such a world because it would be a very good world despite the evil which arises in it. Since premise ii might be false, the conclusion cannot be deduced with logical necessity from the premises. So the argument, as an illative or deductive proof, is flawed.[3] It is important to note that Plantinga is not making the point that ii *is* false; only that it *might be* false. Since it might be false, the conclusion does not necessarily follow from the premises.[4]

Mackie and others have responded by arguing that, even granting that there may be limits to what an omnipotent being can do, it is nonetheless *logically* possible for God to create free agents who do only what is good, and that as an all-powerful and omniscient being, God (if God exists) could bring about a world in which such agents exist. So the question arises again: why didn't God (if there is a God) create human beings who would only freely choose good rather than evil?

Plantinga and others have replied that it may be the case that there are logically possible events or states of affairs regarding human choices that even an omnipotent being cannot bring about. For example, on a widely held understanding of free will – what is often called *libertarian free will* – a person's free choices are truly up to the individual, not something or someone else (even God). So God could not determine the free actions of such individuals. Freedom of this type is incompatible with causal determinism, so God could not cause these free creatures to freely do only what is good, for that would be a logical contradiction.

Furthermore, it can be argued, it is also possible that free will of this robust kind (free will that is incompatible with any sort of determinism) is a very great good. And it may well be that a world containing creatures with this sort of free will is more valuable than a world without such creatures. Consider a world with no free agents whatsoever, one which has only preprogrammed robots, for example. In such a world, the robots would only be acting in ways they are determined to act. Their actions of apparent goodness, kindness and generosity would in fact be actions that were not truly up to them. They would have prior causes that determine them. It seems plausible that the former world – the one with creatures whose choices are truly up to them – is more valuable, all else being equal, than the one with robots and no free creatures. In this more valuable world, however, these free creatures could choose to do evil. That's what it means for an action to be up to the individual: he or she could choose to do good or not. So God may have a morally sufficient reason for not preventing evil completely; evil may be an unavoidable consequence of a very good world.

Another argument raised in support of the logical problem of evil is that, while the free will defense may succeed in undercutting the claim that *moral* evil is inconsistent with the existence of God, it does not address the problem of *natural* evil. The evils of nature are not brought about by the choices of free creatures. So, granting that it may be the case that God (if God exists) should respect the free will of creatures and allow them to choose to do good or evil, God need not allow the *evils of nature* to exist. Countless examples could be cited here: earthquakes that devastate towns or villages; tsunamis that kill tens of thousands of people; forest fires caused by lightning that ravage flora and fauna, and so forth. Other examples are a bit more contentious, but are nevertheless often cited as cases of natural evil, such as predation (organisms or animals maintaining life by killing and feeding on other organisms or animals) and the evolutionary process of natural selection. Aren't these events incompatible with the existence of an all-powerful and perfectly good God?

Plantinga's response is to suggest that it is at least logically possible that perhaps free, non-human persons are responsible for natural evils. Such non-human persons might include rebellious spirits. In some traditional Jewish, Christian and Islamic accounts of the world, this is precisely the case. God created non-human beings, called angels, with free will. Some of these angelic beings turned against God and have been wreaking havoc on the world since its inception. This may even include wreaking havoc on the very processes of evolution. As long as these states of affairs are logical possibilities, the claim that the existence of God and natural evils are logically inconsistent is rebutted.

It will no doubt strike most readers as bizarre that in order to rebut the logical argument from evil, one must resort to positing demons as the cause of natural evil! Strange though it may be, it should be kept in mind that most theists who make use of the free will defense, Plantinga included, do not claim to actually believe this to be the case. They just note that the logic of this argument from evil is not as airtight as its defenders maintain. There are other possibilities. Unlike claims 3 and 4, then, 1 and 2 need not be logically contradictory. God and evil can logically coexist.

These rebuttals to the logical argument from evil have been quite effective. In fact, most theists and atheists now agree that the logical argument has been decisively rebutted. For example, leading atheist philosopher William Rowe states:

> Some philosophers have contended that the existence of evil is *logically inconsistent* with the existence of the theistic God. No one, I think, has succeeded in establishing such an extravagant claim. Indeed, granted incompatibilism [that free will and determinism are incompatible], there is a fairly compelling argument for the view that the existence of evil is logically consistent with the existence of the theistic God.[5]

Agnostic philosopher Paul Draper agrees that the logical problem of evil doesn't work. He argues that the first premise of the argument is problematic. Again, the first premise is this: 'A wholly good being always eliminates evil as far as it can.' Draper maintains that this claim is problematic, for in order to be true it must be demonstrated that God has no morally good reason to allow any particular evil to exist. But establishing that the existence of a particular evil and the existence of God are incompatible cannot be accomplished. Draper puts it this way:

> To understand why this is so [that is, why the existence of a particular evil and God are not necessarily incompatible], it is crucial to understand that the inability to produce things like round squares that are logically impossible to produce or to know statements like $2 + 3 = 10$ that are logically impossible to know does not count as a *lack* of power or a *lack* of knowledge. In other words, not even an all-powerful and all-knowing being can have more power or more knowledge than it is logically possible for a being to have. Suppose, then, that some good, G, that is worth my suffering ... logically implies that I suffer (or that God permits me to suffer). This certainly seems possible ... Such goods would be known to an all-knowing being even if they are beyond our ken. Further, if there are such goods, then not even an all-powerful and all-knowing being could produce them without allowing me to suffer and hence even an all-powerful and all-knowing being could have a good moral reason to permit my suffering.[6]

Since one cannot establish the truth of premise i, the argument cannot get off the ground. So he concurs that the argument is stymied: 'I do not see how it is possible to construct a convincing logical argument from evil against theism.'[7]

The rebuttals to the logical argument, as important as they are, do not put an end to the discussion of evil, however, nor do they solve all the problems related to God and evil. Far from it. Challenges to the existence and goodness of God given evil and suffering have in recent times shifted from the strong claim that theism is *necessarily* false given evil to the more reserved claim that theism (as traditionally understood) is *probably* false given the kind and amount of evil there is in the world. This kind of challenge has a variety of forms which attempt to demonstrate not that claims 1 and 2 are logically incompatible, but rather that it is more reasonable to believe there is no God given the reality of evil than to believe that God exists.

Evidential problems

William Rowe's evidential argument

Evidential arguments attempt to demonstrate that the existence of evil in the world counts as inductive evidence against the claim that God exists. One form of the evidential argument from evil – one considered by many to be the most persuasive – is based on the assumption, often agreed on by theists and atheists alike, that an omnipotent, omniscient, omnibenevolent being would prevent the existence of gratuitous or meaningless evil. The most widely known formulation of this argument is offered by William Rowe:

(i) There exist instances of intense suffering which an omnipotent, omniscient being could have prevented without thereby losing some greater good or permitting some evil equally bad or worse.

(ii) An omnipotent, wholly good being would prevent the occurrence of any intense suffering it could, unless it could not do so without thereby losing some greater good or permitting some evil equally bad or worse.

(iii) Therefore, there does not exist an omnipotent, omniscient, wholly good being.[8]

Rowe maintains that this is an evidential or probabilistic argument since premise (i) is probably true (he believes), though not decisive. If the first premise is probably true, since premise (ii) is true by definition (most theists and atheists accept this claim), it follows that the conclusion is probably true: God probably does not exist.

At first glance it seems that theists and atheists would agree with both premises. Since this argument is valid in form, if one agrees with the two premises, the conclusion follows: an omnipotent, omniscient and omnibenevolent being (probably) does not exist. Rowe offers a particular example of natural evil to support this claim. The example includes a fawn affectionately called 'Bambi' that experiences pointless and terrible suffering in a forest fire which leads to its death. He describes the situation this way:

> Consider again the case of the fawn's suffering. Is it reasonable to believe that there is some greater good so intimately connected to

that suffering that even an omnipotent, omniscient being could not have obtained that good without permitting that suffering or some evil at least as bad? It certainly does not appear reasonable to believe this. Nor does it seem reasonable to believe that there is some evil at least as bad as the fawn's suffering such that an omnipotent being simply could not have prevented it without permitting the fawn's suffering. But even if it should somehow be reasonable to believe either of these things of the fawn's suffering, we must then ask whether it is reasonable to believe either of these things of *all* the instances of seemingly pointless human and animal suffering that occur daily in our world. And surely the answer to this more general question must be no.[9]

Rowe's question of whether an omnipotent, omniscient being could have prevented the fawn's apparently pointless suffering should be haunting for the theist. For, Rowe adds, surely such a being 'could have easily prevented the fawn from being horribly burned, or, given the burning, could have spared the fawn the intense suffering by quickly ending its life, rather than allowing the fawn to lie in terrible agony for several days'.[10] Here is a case, then, that is representative of countless examples of suffering which actually occur in the world, and this gives reason to believe that premise (i) is probably true. The poor fawn's painful death does not seem to be a necessary condition for some greater good. Since it is likely that (i) and (ii) are true, the conclusion that God does not exist is also probably true.

Theists have responded to this argument in various ways. A few have challenged premise (ii), but most agree with it. So the debate generally centres on the first premise. Some claim that there are good reasons to believe that premise (i) is false, while others claim that we are not in an appropriate epistemic (knowledge) position to know that premise (i) is true. The first approach generally involves *theodicy* – the attempt to justify God and the ways of God given the evil and suffering in the world. We will explore several theodicies in the next chapter. A second approach involves questioning the reasons one might affirm premise (i). Rowe asks if it is 'reasonable to believe that there is some greater good so intimately connected to that [fawn's] suffering that even an omnipotent, omniscient being could not have obtained that good without permitting that suffering or some evil at least as bad?'. His conclusion is that it certainly does not appear reasonable to believe so. Since there *does not appear* to be any good or any sufficient reason for affirming so, he maintains, there probably is not one. What are we to make of this claim?

Noseeum arguments and skeptical theism

It is no doubt true that sometimes when something does not appear, we can reasonably conclude that it does not exist. However, it is also true that the inference 'does not exist' from 'does not appear' is not always a good one to make. Stephen Wykstra has called arguments such as this 'noseeum arguments', and they take this form: as far as we can surmise, there are no Xs; therefore, there are no Xs. In Rowe's argument it is alleged that after carefully looking for a greater good that might come about from some gratuitous evil (such as the suffering and death of Bambi), none can be found. So it is reasonable to conclude that there are none.[11] But is this a plausible inference?

Noseeum arguments can be strong or weak, good or bad. Suppose a friend told you that, after carefully studying the stars, she believes that you will soon win a lot of money. After examining her alleged astrological evidence for this claim (horoscopes and Tarot cards), it doesn't seem to you that what she says is reasonable to believe. You don't see any real evidence in what she has presented to you, and you have reason to believe that astrology of this sort is suspect. In this case, your noseeum inference that her claim is false is a good one. But consider another example. Suppose that you go to an alternative health practitioner with a terrible pain in your chest. The 'doctor' takes a careful look at your eyes and says that nothing seems amiss. You inquire about the significance of looking at eyes for heart conditions, ask about further medical testing, such as an electrocardiogram, chest X-ray, or stress test – even a stethoscope would be good! But he says that since he doesn't see anything wrong in your eyes, no further testing is necessary. He concludes that your heart is quite healthy. In this case, the noseeum inference is a bad one.

So what about the atheist's inference from evil? Is it more like the first example or the second? Some theists, including those affirming what's called *skeptical theism* (skeptical theists are theists who are skeptical about a human being's ability to make informed judgements about what God has done or would do in any particular situation), claim that the atheist's inference is like the second. This is akin to the words of the Hebrew prophet Isaiah who, speaking on behalf of God, says the following: 'For my thoughts are not your thoughts, nor are your ways my ways, says the Lord. For as the heavens are higher than the earth, so are my ways higher than your ways and my thoughts than your thoughts' (55.8-9).

God's ways are inscrutable, so we are in no position to judge as improbable the claim that there are great goods secured by God through the various evils which exist. There may well be many great goods brought about by evil acts which we cannot comprehend, given our cognitive (and other) limitations. And there may be other good reasons for allowing evil. Since God's ways are so far beyond the ability of finite minds to grasp, we are simply not justified in affirming that there are evils which have no point, even though they may appear to us this way. An analogy may help. I was recently playing chess with my ten-year-old son. He's a novice at the game (I must admit that I'm no expert myself, but I am several years advanced beyond him!), and he failed to understand why I made a certain move in the game. At first he thought the move was wrongheaded and that I had made a detrimental mistake. But alas, I proved him wrong. Given his limited understanding of chess, he was not in an appropriate epistemic place to conclude that the move was pointless. He was simply not able to recognize its purpose.[12]

Something akin to this claim emerges in another place in the Bible. In the book of Job, after suffering great personal harm and loss, Job demands a response from God. 'Then the Lord answered Job ... "Who is this that darkens my counsel by words without knowledge? .... Where were you when I laid the foundation of the earth? Tell me if you have understanding. Who determined its measurements ... ?"' (38:1-4). As the questioning continues, Job is brought to silence before God, for he realizes the depths of his own cognitive limitations with respect to God and the creation. He finally responds: 'I know that you can do all things ... Therefore, I have uttered what I did not understand, things too wonderful for me, which I did not know' (42.2-3).

In Islam, too, the inscrutable ways of God is a prominent theme. In the Qur'an, surah 2.155-57, we find these words:

Be sure we shall test you with something of fear and hunger, some loss in goods or lives or the fruits (of your toil), but give glad tidings to those who patiently persevere, Who say, when afflicted with calamity: 'To God We belong, and to Him is our return.' They are those on whom (Descend) blessings from God, and Mercy, and they are the ones that receive guidance.

We do not know the wisdom behind the occurrences of evil and suffering in our lives; we cannot obtain a proper perspective on such complex matters, for our minds are so far from the greatness of Allah's infinite mind that to suppose we could understand such matters would be pure hubris. In faith, we turn to God, and we trust that he is both just and good.

Perhaps the most persuasive argument for skeptical theism, CORNEA, was offered by Wykstra. CORNEA is an acronym for the Condition on Reasonable Epistemic Access. According to this argument, inferences from 'I see no X' to 'There is no X' are justified only if it is reasonable, all things considered, for one to believe that if there were in fact an X, one would be likely to see X. For example, in following the CORNEA strategy, the inference from 'I see nothing wrong in your eyes' to 'Your heart is fine' would not pass muster. Similarly, skeptical theists argue, the inference from 'As far as we can surmise, there is no compensating good for this or that particular evil (or set of evils)' to 'God does not exist' does not pass muster either. There are simply too many variables of which we are unfamiliar to make such assessments.

Consider another example which drives home the point. Those working in the field of chaos theory have discovered that the slightest perturbations of the early conditions of a dynamical system can have significant effects on larger systems which would have been impossible to predict given empirical observations. Reflecting on this, William Lane Craig makes the following point:

> I want to argue that we're just not in a good position to assess the probability of whether God lacks morally sufficient reasons for permitting the evils that occur. Take an analogy from chaos theory. In chaos theory, scientists tell us that even the flutter of a butterfly's wings could produce forces that would set in motion causes that would produce a hurricane over the Atlantic Ocean. And yet looking at that butterfly palpitating on a branch, it is impossible in principle to predict such an outcome. Similarly, an evil in the world, say, a child's dying of cancer or a brutal murder of a man,

could set a ripple effect in history going, such that God's morally sufficient reason for permitting it might not emerge until centuries later or maybe in another country. We're just not in a position to be able to make these kinds of probability judgments.[13]

There have been a number of responses to skeptical theism, including Rowe's argument that for the skeptical theist there could never be *any* reason for doubting God's existence given evil, no matter how horrific and extensive it may be. The skeptical theist, he argues, has made the divide between divine knowledge and human knowledge too wide – wider than what theism affirms. While a modified view of God which widens the human/divine cognitive chasm may suffice as a response to premise (i), *theism* per se does not. In other words, Rowe maintains, Wykstra has unjustifiably imported the further notions of God's mysterious and incomprehensible purposes and human cognitive limitations into the argument, which renders it invalid as stated. Rowe makes a good point, but the theist of the Abrahamic faiths need not see this as a liability, for the human limitations and inscrutability of God propounded by Wykstra are and historically have been widely held among theologians of these traditions.

Paul Draper's evidential argument

A recent move by Paul Draper has advanced the discussion of the evidential argument. He argues that the world as it is, with its distribution of pains and pleasures, is more likely given what he calls a 'hypothesis of indifference' than given theism. On the hypothesis of indifference, 'neither the nature nor the condition of sentient beings on earth is the result of benevolent or malevolent actions performed by nonhuman persons'.[14] On the theistic account, since God is morally perfect there must be morally good reasons for allowing biologically useless pain, and there must be morally good reasons for producing pleasures even if such pleasures are not biologically useful. But given our observations of the pains and pleasures experienced by sentient creatures, including their biologically gratuitous experiences, the hypothesis of indifference provides a more reasonable account than theism. This alternative hypothesis to theism, in other words, is more likely to be true than the theistic one.

However, this argument can be countered by contending that for all we know, in every possible world which exhibits a high degree of complexity – a world such as ours with sentient, intelligent life – the laws of nature are the same or have the same general features as our actual laws. So we cannot assume that the distribution of pain and pleasure in a world with a high degree of complexity such as ours, including the pains and pleasures reflected in biological evolution, would be any different given theism. We are simply not in an epistemic position to assign a reliable probability either way, so we cannot make the judgement that theism is less likely than the hypothesis of indifference.

Up to this point it has been assumed that the theist carries the burden of proof. But the question can be raised whether the theist does, after all, hold the burden, or whether other positions share an equal burden, or whether indeed other positions have more of a burden. Perhaps this is a case where issues of worldview are relevant, for if one has reasons for affirming atheism prior to attending to cases of apparently gratuitous evil, then it may well be that the burden lies with the theist to demonstrate how such cases of evil can be justified given theism. On the other hand, if one has reasons for affirming theism prior to attending to cases of apparently gratuitous evil, perhaps the burden of proof lies with the atheist to demonstrate how such cases of evil cannot be justified given theism. And if one has reasons for affirming some other worldview – Hinduism, say – then perhaps the burden is placed elsewhere. Furthermore, it may well be that the atheist or the Hindu (or what have you) has his or her own challenges with respect to the reality of evil and suffering. These are important issues that we will pick up in Chapters 5 and 6.

Concluding reflections

The problems of evil spelled out in this chapter are major objections that have been levelled against belief in God given the reality of evil in the world. They are indeed troubling arguments for theists and cannot be easily dismissed. I have had many discussions with theists who attempt to trivialize the problems of evil (with atheists, too, but that will come up in a later chapter), but then further into the dialogue realize they have not really explored the theoretical dimensions of the problems. The difficulties are significant, and they should not be minimized. As we have seen, though, they are not necessarily so formidable as to make belief in a morally perfect and powerful deity illogical or rationally unwarranted.

At this point, we have only explored responses to the theoretical problems of evil – what are frequently called *defenses* in which the scenarios depicted are logically possible ones. We have not yet explored any attempts to *justify* God and the ways of God given the evil and suffering that exists in the world. That is to say, we have not yet explored *theodicy* in which the scenarios depicted in the explanations are offered as true ones. The next chapter moves us into the heart of such attempts.

Further reading

Adams, Marilyn M. and Robert M. Adams. 1990. *The Problem of Evil*. New York: Oxford University Press. (A scholarly collection of essays from a variety of perspectives by leading philosophers.)

Ahmud, Isham. 2011. 'The Problem of Evil in Islam and Christianity: Suffering from the Philosophical Perspectives in Medieval Thought,' *International Journal of the Humanities* 6(11): 101–10.

Feinberg, John S. (2004), *The Many Faces of Evil: Theological Systems and the Problem of Evil*. 3rd ed. Wheaton, IL: Crossway.

Hume, David. 1955. *Dialogues Concerning Natural Religion*, ed. Henry David Aiken. Parts 10 and 11. New York: Hafner Publishing.

Lewis, Clive Staples. 1962. *The Problem of Pain*. New York: Macmillan. (Lewis focuses on the value of pain and suffering as God's 'megaphone' to rouse a morally deaf world.)

Mackie, John L. 1982. *The Miracle of Theism*. Oxford: Clarendon Press. (See especially his chapter on the problem of evil.)

Martin, Michael. 1990. *Atheism*. Philadelphia, PA: Temple University Press. (Includes a wide-ranging critique of theistic responses to the problem of evil; note especially chapters 14–17.)

Plantinga, Alvin. 1977. *God, Freedom and Evil*. Grand Rapids, MI: Eerdmans. (A classic account of the free will defense.)

CHAPTER THREE

Theodicy

So far we have investigated various problems of evil that confront theists. While these are indeed serious objections to belief in a beneficent and all-powerful deity, in the previous chapter I argued that religious adherents need not be unreasonable in their belief that God exists despite these objections, for there are plausible rebuttals to them, even if they are only logically possible scenarios. Some theists are satisfied to leave it there. God is God, and who are we to question? God and God's ways are beyond our understanding. Other theists are not so satisfied with merely having responses to evil that might be true. Instead, they want to know whether there are greater goods that actually justify the evil, pain and suffering in the world. They are looking for answers that in fact are, or at least probably are, true. This is the role of theodicy.

A theodicy is different from a defense. The aim of a defense is to demonstrate that the arguments from evil are unsuccessful given a possible scenario or set of scenarios, whereas the aim of a theodicy is to justify God and the ways of God in a world filled with evil. A theodicy takes on the burden of attempting to vindicate God by providing a plausible explanation for evil. Theodicy often takes the following general form:

God, an omnipotent and omnibenevolent being, will prevent/ eliminate evil unless there is a good reason or set of reasons for not doing so.
There is evil in the world.
Therefore, God must have a good reason or set of reasons for not preventing/eliminating evil.

There are a variety of attempts to demonstrate what that good reason is, or those good reasons are, for the reality of evil in the world. Two of the most prominent are the free will and soul-making theodicies. We will first explore them before examining what I shall call a theodicy of fulfilment – a view that takes into consideration important factors absent from the other two.

A free will theodicy

The most prominent theodicy historically is one formulated by St. Augustine sometime around the early fifth century ce. Augustine has been one of the most influential Christian philosophers/theologians of the Western world. His spiritual pilgrimage included evolving from scepticism as a young adult to Christian Bishop of Hippo in his later years. His writings on human free will, which are central to his understanding of evil, spanned his career, and virtually every medieval philosopher of renown in the Christian West interacted with his work on this subject.

Augustine spent much time thinking about and writing on the subject of evil. From his earlier works, including *On the Free Choice of the Will*, to his more mature works, *The City of God* and the *Confessions*, and many works in between, he continually turned to the notion of evil. Two central questions were at the heart of his thinking on the subject: 1) What is the nature of evil? and 2) Where does evil come from? Augustine affirmed the commonly held Hebrew–Christian view of the world that it was created by God and was good, very good. Everything that God created is fundamentally good and has a good purpose. But evil is also a real part of this world, so what is it? And how did it arise?

Augustine's answer is rooted in the thinking of the philosopher Plotinus who lived in the third century. It was then picked up by Augustine more than a century later and has been a significant part of Christian thinking on the matter ever since. Augustine argued that while God is indeed the creator of everything, evil is not a thing; it is a *privatio boni* – a privation of the good. By 'privation' Plotinus and Augustine meant the absence of a thing. To clarify this idea, Augustine used the example of a person who is blind. Blindness is not in itself a thing – not a substantial reality – let alone a good thing. It is a privation of seeing. Evil, he argues, is like blindness.

It is a lack of good. But we are still left with the question that if God created a very good world, what brought about the evil? How did it arise in the world if not from the creator of the world? For Augustine, the state of the world in which human beings first found themselves was one of absolute perfection and goodness. But unlike its unlimited and immutable creator, it is finite and changeable. It was this mutability, this potential for change, that opened the door to privation and corruption.

Augustine's narrative begins with the creation of the Garden of Eden, an idyllic paradise in which there was no evil, no suffering, and no pain. Adam and Eve were created *ex nihilo*, out of nothing, and placed in the Garden in a state of moral perfection. So how did evil emerge in such a blissful state? The story is a familiar one. Some of God's creation, most notably this first human pair, was created in God's image. This image reflected God in creativity, love and moral choice. But at some point along the way, the will of these free persons turned from God, the *summum bonum* (supreme good), to lesser goods. This turning of the will from God and the supreme good to lesser goods was the origin of evil, and it ushered in further evil into the world. In Christian theology, ever since Augustine, this event has been referred to as the Fall. It happened first with the angels, spearheaded by Satan (the supreme fallen angel), and then, after being tempted by him, with the first human couple. For Augustine, this turning of the will explains the moral evil in the world. This moral fall, or sin, brought with it not only guilt, shame and punishment for human beings, but also tragic cosmic consequences, for it marshalled into the universe all manner of pain and suffering. It also brought with it divine punishment. God's punishment, then, accounts for much of the natural evil in the world; natural evils are the effects of sin and divine wrath. The Fall, then, was no insignificant event. It was a disaster of cataclysmic proportions and accounts for all of the moral and natural evil in the world.

Augustine's theodicy does not end without resolution, however. For in the eschaton – in the end of the world as we know it – God will rectify matters when he judges the world in righteousness, ushering into God's eternal kingdom those persons who have been saved through the atoning work of Christ and sending to eternal perdition those persons who are wicked and disobedient. Augustine's theodicy can be summarized this way:

1   God created the universe and everything in it was good; the first humans were placed in a perfect paradise.

2   Some of God's creation – namely persons – were given the good gift of freedom of the will (having freedom of the will in the universe is better than not having it, since a moral universe requires it, and a moral universe is better than a non-moral one).

3   Some of these created persons – first angels, and then human beings – freely chose to turn from God and the good; that is, they 'sinned' and fell from their state of moral and spiritual perfection; this is the 'Fall'.

4   This turning of the will, or sin, ushered into the world all manner of moral and natural evil.

5   There are two dimensions to evil: a) its origin, which is misdirected will and b) its nature, which is metaphysical deprivation, or privation, of the good.

6   God will eventually rectify matters by bringing evil to an end when he judges the world in righteousness, marshalling into God's eternal kingdom those persons who have been saved through Christ and sending to eternal hell those persons who are wicked and disobedient.

This has been the most prominent theodicy since its inception in the fifth century, and is still widely held in one form or another today.

While this free will theodicy does, in one sense, exonerate God from evil by placing responsibility for it upon creatures God created, and while it has been extensively advocated by theists for centuries, it has been highly criticized in recent times. One problem with it is the question that, even granting a robust libertarian view of free will, could God not have prevented the consequences of the evil decisions made by free creatures – consequences having to do with both moral and natural evils? To list some specific examples, could God not have prevented the earthquake in Haiti in 2010 in which over 200,000 people died and over a million were left homeless? Could God not have stopped the Black Plague in the fourteenth century that wiped out well over 30 percent of Europe's population? And while perhaps not being able to avert members of the Nazi regime from freely deciding to torture and execute millions of Jews, or Joseph Stalin's collectivization policy in which millions of peasants died, could God not have orchestrated events in such a way that totalitarian leaders such as these failed in their attempts, thus preventing the massive and horrific manslaughters of the past and present? In other words, while this theodicy may account for some of the moral and natural evils that exist, it does not seem to provide an answer for why there is so much evil, and why there is so much evil which seems utterly horrific and gratuitous.

Furthermore, would not a world without free will be better than a world with free will if evil of this magnitude is its result? Maybe. But free will certainly seems to be a great value, and perhaps this value is great enough that God is perfectly justified in not thwarting the consequences of bad events, even if they are horrific. How could a person love another without free will? How could meaningful relationships exist without the freedom to choose? Perhaps there is value in the experiences that occur in individuals because of evil events. And how do we know that there are not greater goods that result from evil actions – goods which would not have arisen without them, including the virtues of compassion, mercy and courage? This of course brings up the issue addressed in the previous chapter regarding skeptical theism. It does seem reasonable, if not likely, that we are simply not intellectually capable of making fully informed judgements about situations of this sort. It may well be that the complexities of our world are too vast and multifarious for finite minds to understand how there could be moral justification for great evils.

There is another problem, however, which has been raised again St. Augustine's free will theodicy given modern scientific understandings of the biological and social development of Homo sapiens. It no longer seems very reasonable to believe that human beings began in a state of moral and spiritual maturity and perfection (a view usually associated with the notion that the universe began about 6,000 years ago) and then fell into a state of moral depravity as depicted in Augustine's notion of the Fall and original sin and a strictly literal interpretation of the early chapters of the book of Genesis. The story of human history is now widely understood by the scientific community to be one of evolutionary development and moral and social progress rather than the devolution depicted in some conservative and fundamentalist interpretations of the biblical creation account. Human civilization seems to have been advancing over the last hundred thousand years or so, and this advancement has included biological and moral progress. Looking back at just the last several millennia, for example, it is doubtful that many people today would be happy to return to the moral imperatives of the Old Testament or the Code of Hammurabi, or to the legal status of women and minority groups which were maintained throughout most of recorded human history.

Furthermore, many of the hard sciences, including geology, paleobiology and genetics, have demonstrated that natural evils existed long before the emergence of human life, or any conscious life for that matter, and so could not have been the consequence of misdirected human will. It seems clear that evil, at least in the form of suffering and pain, existed long before human beings ever did. This is perhaps the most devastating objection to Augustine's theodicy, for it could not have been that human choice brought about all the evil and misery that exists in the world. This doesn't doom every aspect of the theodicy, however. Free will can still play a significant role in theodicy. Maybe, for example, the first Homo sapiens developed moral awareness and made choices that had significant moral consequences. Evolution does not necessarily negate the existence of a first pair of morally free hominids. But it does contradict the notion that humans began in a perfectly good moral state a short time ago in world history and are responsible (along with fallen angels) for all the moral and natural evil that exists in our world.

In sum, Augustine's theodicy as he developed it is incongruent with modern science, but his intuition of the role of free will in theodicy need not necessarily be jettisoned. Another attempt at theodicy includes this central element of free will but provides an overall better fit with the latest scientific accounts of the natural world and its history.

A soul-making theodicy

Based on the work of the early Christian theologian Irenaeus (c. 130–c. 202 CE), as well as insights from the nineteenth-century German theologian F. D. E. Schleiermacher, John Hick has developed a theodicy which stands, in some ways, in stark contrast to Augustine's approach. Hick argues that his theodicy is more plausible given contemporary sensibilities rooted in science and the most up-to-date scholarship in religion, the history of religion, and other disciplines. In Hick's view, God did not create a paradise 6,000 years ago with perfect human beings who then misused their free will and so brought about a grand moral and metaphysical defect in the universe. Instead, God created the universe billions of years ago as a good place – a place of value, purpose and meaning – but no paradise, for developing morally mature human beings. Through Darwinian processes, morally aware conscious beings would evolve out of inert, impersonal matter. The first such beings would reflect brute selfishness and self-centredness but would eventually have the opportunity, through struggle and choice, to advance to a higher state of moral and spiritual maturity. The world is thus a grand soul-making environment, and such an environment requires challenge and struggle. 'God's purpose,' as Hick puts it,

> ... was not to construct a paradise whose inhabitants would experience a maximum of pleasure and a minimum of pain. The world is seen, instead, as a place of 'soul making' or person making in which free beings, grappling with the tasks and challenges of their existence in a common environment, may become 'children of God' and 'heirs of eternal life'. Our world, with all its rough edges, is the sphere in which this second and harder stage of the creative process is taking place.[1]

The problem with a paradise world, such as the one depicted in the Garden of Eden story in which there is no possibility of struggle – no pain and suffering and hardship – is that saintliness may be unattainable in a world like that. There are elements of struggle and difficulty that seem to be necessary for moral growth. In a paradise world,

> No one would ever injure anyone else; the murderer's knife would turn to paper or his bullets to thin air; the bank safe, robbed of a million dollars, would miraculously become filled with another million dollars; fraud, deceit, conspiracy, and treason would somehow always leave the fabric of society undamaged ... The reckless driver would never meet with disaster. There would be no need to work, since no harm could result from avoiding work; there would be no call to be concerned for others in time of need or danger, for in such a world there could be no real needs or dangers.[2]

In a world of no real needs, dangers or difficulties, many virtues such as courage, compassion and generosity would be completely absent. If God desired to bring about creatures who reflected such virtues, evil, it seems, would be a necessary component. Evil then, argues Hick, is not the result of perfect persons choosing to sin, but rather is an inevitable aspect of an environment that is necessary for developing persons of mature moral character. By placing evolving beings in the demanding, even fractious environment of our world, through their ability to choose what is right and good they can gradually develop into the mature persons that God desires them to be, exhibiting such virtues as courage, honesty, compassion and selfless love.

This soul-making (or 'person-making') theodicy contains the element of free will that the Augustinian theodicy had, but it places the role of free will in the midst of evolving persons over eons of time rather than in two perfect persons who lived a rather short time ago. Hick's theodicy also has God continuing his efforts in the development of human persons even in the afterlife by allowing them non-coercive opportunities to love and choose the good so that eventually everyone will have the opportunity to experience moral perfection and so be brought into a full and proper relationship with God. In this view, because of the universal love of God, every person may, and probably will, ultimately experience redemption.

To summarize the soul-making theodicy, God created a world that includes evil, suffering and hardship for the purpose of developing morally and spiritually mature persons. The process has taken billions of years, beginning with unconscious matter, and it won't be completed until some distant time in the future when human persons (and perhaps other types of persons) will have reached moral maturity. We can delineate this theodicy as follows:

1   God created the world as a good place, but no paradise, for developing human persons both spiritually and morally.
2   Through evolutionary means, God brought about such persons who have the freedom of will and the capacity to mature in love and goodness.
3   By placing human persons in this challenging environment, through their own free responses they have the opportunity to choose what is right and good and thus grow into the mature persons that God desires them to be (exhibiting the virtues of patience, courage, generosity and so on).
4   Evil is the result of both the creation of a soul-making world and of the human choice to sin.
5   God will continue to work with human (and perhaps other) persons, even in the afterlife as necessary, by allowing them

opportunities to love and choose the good so that in the eschaton everyone may be brought into a place of moral and spiritual maturity.

There is a simplicity and elegance to this theodicy, and it meshes well with the current evolutionary account of the world. At first blush, though, it is overshadowed by a major objection: while it may be true that a soul-making environment cannot be a paradise, the degree and extent of pain and suffering which exist in the world are surely unjustified. Why did there have to be an Auschwitz, say, or medieval torture chambers? Why did the Black Plague have to occur? Why the great tsunamis? Could not mature persons be developed without these kinds of horrors? To make matters worse, some evils seem to be character-destroying rather than character-building. Some individuals do not improve through the hardships they endure; oftentimes the difficulties in one's life cause it to end in utter tragedy. Think of a young child with a debilitating disease who is regularly mocked and then dies at an early age; or a woman who is brutally raped, held captive, and then murdered days later; or a mother who backs her minivan out of the garage and inadvertently runs over her young daughter. Or what about the doe who suffers and dies in a forest fire? Do such examples of horrific and apparently gratuitous evil not count against a theodicy like this?

A soul-making theodicist might respond by claiming that apparently pointless evils are not, in fact, without purpose and merit after all. The kinds of sympathy and compassion, for example, that are evoked from such seemingly indiscriminate and unfair miseries are very great goods in and of themselves – goods which would not arise without the miseries appearing as unfair and indiscriminate. Even though God did not intend or need any particular evils, such as Auschwitz, for his soul-making purposes, God did need to create an environment where such evils were a real possibility. So while each individual instance of evil may not be justified by a particular greater good, the existence of a world where evil is possible is necessary for a world where soul-making takes place.

In addition, while there are cases in which difficulties in individuals' lives do breed bitterness, anger, fear, selfishness and a general lessening of virtuous character, if there is an afterlife God could well continue this process of soul-making until a person has had the opportunity to mature. Furthermore, as we will see in the final chapter, an afterlife may also provide future goods which are great enough to justify even the worst horrors experienced in this life.

A theodicy of fulfilment

The two theodicies expressed so far are in agreement about the central role of free will in the emergence and propagation of evil and the advancement of good in human history. But they disagree about how the world has unfolded, particularly with respect to human moral development. In the Augustinian theodicy, human beings were made morally perfect and then fell into sin. In the soul-making view, human beings emerged from lower life forms through eons of biological and moral evolution. As already noted, the soul-making approach is more consonant with contemporary science than the Augustinian one. However, including evolution as a critical aspect of the way God made the world impugns the notion of a good creation, and it appears to make God the author of large amounts of evil in the world. If God established certain parameters of physics and biology so that from inanimate matter living conscious organisms would evolve, then it is God who is responsible for the struggle, suffering and death that are at the very heart of the evolutionary process. In other words, if something like Darwinian evolution is true, God appears to be the creator of a form of natural evil that is at the very heart of natural, biological processes. It is a disconcerting (and quite anthropocentric) claim that the countless living organisms which have suffered and died throughout earth's history were mere evolutionary expedients brought about by God for the purposes of human moral and spiritual development. If something like the soul-making theodicy is to succeed, it needs further development in order to answer this rather serious objection.

Darwinian evolution might be mistaken in some significant way, but let's take it for granted that something akin to Darwin's account of the development of flora and fauna is correct. Biological evolution as understood in contemporary science is the theory of the change of organic species over time. Its central elements include natural selection, mutation and genetic drift. There is currently widespread disagreement among biologists regarding what, precisely, natural selection entails. In essence, though, it is the process in which organisms that have certain genetic characteristics (ones that make them better adjusted to an environment) tend to survive and reproduce, and are therefore better able to perpetuate these characteristics to succeeding generations. Those organisms better adapted to their environment tend to survive; those less adapted tend to be eliminated. Mutations are changes in the DNA sequence of a cell's genome which are caused by such factors as radiation, viruses and errors in DNA replication. These mutations may be harmful to an organism, or they may be beneficial, or they may have no effect at all. The third element, genetic drift, is a change in the gene pool of a small population which occurs by chance. This can result in certain genetic characteristics being lost completely from the gene pool, and unlike natural selection this drifting has nothing to do with the survivability of the organism or population. In nature, then, law and chance are both powerful forces which together bring about the emergence and self-unfolding of ever higher levels of organization which have culminated in sentient, conscious life.

These biological processes are formative in the unfolding of all living organisms on our planet. Given their essential role in world history, the question arises: is there a plausible justification for God's creating a world which includes the effort, opposition, obstruction, aggression, pain, suffering and even death which are characteristics of this world? It has been argued by a number of philosophers and others that the world we live in makes more sense given naturalism (the hypothesis that natural entities have only natural causes and that no supernatural entities, such as God, exist) than theism. Paul Draper, for example, whom we met in Chapter 2, makes such a case. His argument centres on the evolutionary struggle for survival and begins with the following statement:

> For a variety of biological and ecological reasons, organisms compete for survival, with some having an advantage in the struggle for survival over others; as a result, many organisms, including many sentient beings, never flourish because they die before maturity, many others barely survive, but languish for most or all of their lives, and those that reach maturity and flourish for much of their lives usually languish in old age; in the case of human beings and some nonhuman animals as well, languishing often involves intense or prolonged suffering.[3]

He then argues that since we know this claim is true, and that this claim is many times more likely given naturalism than theism, if other evidences are equal, we have strong evidence for naturalism – much more so than for theism. Evolutionist Richard Dawkins also addresses the issue when he says that the world looks exactly as it would if there is 'at bottom, no design, no purpose, no evil and no good, nothing but blind pitiless indifference'.[4] No doubt the pain, suffering and death experienced by sentient creatures because of evolution seem at first blush to reflect anything but the grand design of a perfectly good and omniscient creator.

Could it be that such processes are intrinsic to or even necessary for bringing about the kinds of beauty, diversity, richness, consciousness and moral awareness reflected in our world? Is it possible that such dimensions of reality could not have come to be in a different manner? I think so. In fact, if theism is true, and if the world has indeed evolved through Darwinian principles as noted above, then it may well be that such processes, or something very much like them, are a crucial and perhaps even necessary vehicle for the complexity, beauty, freedom and morality that we experience. In any case, a satisfactory theodicy must take into account these evolutionary processes and the apparently gratuitous evil intrinsic to biological evolution.

In what follows, then, I will sketch a theodicy that includes the main elements of free will and soul-making but also emphasizes a redemptive component which, I believe, is requisite for a morally satisfactory account of the workings of God in the natural world.[5] The core of this theodicy of fulfilment is: God created a good world that brought about many kinds of goods and values, including human persons with moral capacities and dispositions. Free choices that have real moral consequences are an essential feature of moral and spiritual development and maturity for creatures such as ourselves, and God desires our development and maturity. In order for free choices with real moral consequences to be possible, a challenging environment is necessary – one in which good, evil, pain and suffering are not only present but also produce contrary moral dispositions within the moral agent – and this environment in our world includes the processes of biological evolution. Pain and suffering, however, are not mere evolutionary expedients for the moral and spiritual development of human beings; for the world to be truly good, every sentient creature must have the opportunity to experience its own individual fulfilment, if not in this life then certainly in the afterlife. Let's unpack each of these points.

First, goodness is more fundamental than evil, for it is rooted in the reality of God. God is good, and the world God created is also good. It has intrinsic value. But the world was created in inchoate form. Our universe sprang into existence as a singularity roughly 13 billion years ago in an immensely hot and dense state. It then expanded (the 'big bang') and began cooling and forming galaxies. Over eons of time clouds of stellar dust congealed into stars and planets. At least one of those planets (but perhaps countless others) fell into planetary habitability where the conditions were just right for carbon-based life. Through a variety of inexplicable processes, life emerged on this planet and developed into higher and higher life forms. This created world was, then, intrinsically good and filled with value, and through natural processes it brought forth further values and goods – including the vast variety of living creatures which have existed and do exist and culminating, as it were, in Homo sapiens: sentient creatures with the capacity to make moral choices.

Furthermore goodness, as commonly understood in Western philosophy and theology, encompasses all moral perfection, including benevolence – willing the benefit of another. God wills the good of all creation. In the Abrahamic faiths, one expression of divine benevolence is redemption – transforming persons into new life with God. While the emphasis of redemption in these traditions has generally been on persons, there is nothing inherent in them which excludes the potential redemption, the transformation, of all sentient beings.

The next point of this theodicy is that for moral development to occur, moral agents must have the ability to make choices, and these choices must have real moral consequences. Arguably, for there to be this kind of choice it must be free, and free in a robust sense. In other words, it must be the kind of freedom that is incompatible with determinism. This type of free will, called libertarian free will, as we saw in the last chapter, involves individual control over one's choices and actions. For libertarian freedom, a person exercises her or his own causal powers when acting freely so that when a free choice is made, nothing determines that choice except the person's own act of will. For example, when I type on the keypad that is before me, I am choosing which words to put on this page. I could have chosen other words, or I could have chosen not to write at all.

This sort of free will may seem to contradict the omnipotence of God, for human free choices are not caused by God, they are caused by human persons, and sometimes they even go against the will of God. This power of choice doesn't actually contradict divine omnipotence, however, if by omnipotence we mean maximal power. For even if God has maximal power, it does not follow that God has the ability to do anything conceivable. As we explored in the first chapter, there are many things that God cannot do. God cannot make it the case that $2 + 2 = 5$, nor can God create a square circle. So, too, it may well be that God cannot create a world of perfectly mature, moral human persons without those persons making free choices and developing through the ramifications of those choices. For just as it makes no sense to believe that God can make square circles (the very notion of a square circle is incoherent, so there is no such thing as a square circle for God to create), so too it makes no sense to believe that God could create by divine fiat morally mature, perfect persons who do only what is right and good. Moral maturity requires that moral agents be involved in the formation of their character through the arduous process of moral decision-making.

This leads to the third point. To make free choices of the type that have real moral merit, a proper environment is necessary. Moral decision-making occurs within particular contexts, and it seems that a proper context for real moral choice is one which includes opposing desires or dispositions within the individual making the choice. Consider this example. Suppose you have some extra cash on hand and are confronted with the decision of whether to (a) send money to a starving child in a poverty-stricken land (a friend, say, brought the child to your attention) or (b) use the money to purchase a new unnecessary gadget to go along with your brand new laptop computer. If there were no competing desires within you, say one of selfish ambition and another of altruistic generosity (both of which are intrinsic features of biological evolution which have emerged through conflict and struggle), what would the choice at hand consist of? It seems that with the felt qualities of the conflicting desires we experience, real choice makes more sense. So, internal conflicts are a necessary part of the very nature of moral development, at least in the early phases of individual moral formation. In *Harry Potter and the Order of the Phoenix*, Sirius Black makes a relevant point: 'The world isn't split into good people and death eaters. We've all got both light and dark inside of us. What matters is the part we choose to act on. That's who we really are.' I believe this is right. And, I would add, that's who we really become.

So a life lived making moral choices, deciding between opposing intrinsic or innate dispositions and desires, is an essential part of the transformation of one's character into one that is morally mature. If it is the case that competing desires and dispositions are requisite for moral decision-making (at least in its developmental phase), then something akin to aggression, disappointment, frustration, danger and pain – all of which are essential features of biological evolution – are in fact necessary for real moral progress to occur. Perhaps, then, the natural evils we see in biological evolution are essential elements of an otherwise unattainable and very great good.

The final point of this theodicy is that, even though God has chosen to use evolution as the primary vehicle for the creation and maturation of living organisms, God would not bring about a world with creatures who experience evil for purposes of mere evolutionary expediency. It would be highly anthropocentric to affirm that the natural world, with its suffering, death and predation, exists only for the advanced development of human moral perfection – as mere preparation for the development of moral and spiritual virtue among humans. All creatures are valuable, and all creatures, at least all sentient ones, should experience eschatological fulfilment. This means that every creature has the opportunity to experience its own flourishing, either in this life or in the next.

The importance of the eschatological fulfllment of all sentient creatures is not a new idea. Keith Ward offered the following insight decades ago:

> Theism would be falsified if physical death was the end, for then there could be no justification for the existence of this world. However, if one supposes that every sentient being has an endless existence, which offers the prospect of supreme happiness, it is surely true that the sorrows and troubles of this life will seem very small in comparison. Immortality, for animals as well as humans, is a necessary condition of any acceptable theodicy; that necessity, together with all the other arguments for God, is one of the main reasons for believing in immortality.[6]

Neither did the idea begin with Professor Ward. Long before him, John Wesley shared a similar sentiment in responding to the claim that there might be an objection made against God for the suffering of so many animals: 'But the objection vanishes away if we consider that something better remains after death for these creatures also; that these likewise shall one day be delivered from this bondage of corruption, and shall then receive an ample amends for all their present sufferings.'[7] And long before Wesley, the biblical author of the book of Colossians intimated such fulfilment: 'For God was pleased to have all his fullness dwell in him [Christ], and through him to reconcile to himself *all things*, whether things on earth or things in heaven, by making peace through his blood, shed on the cross' (NRSV, chapter 1, verses 19-20; italics added). But the idea didn't originate with the New Testament, either. We find the Hebrew prophets reflecting on a future time when suffering and predation will be no more and humans and animals will experience life redeemed:

> The wolf will live with the lamb,
> The leopard will lie down with the goat,
> The calf and the lion and the yearling together;
> A little child will lead them.
> The cow will feed with the bear,
> Their young will lie down together,
> And the lion will eat straw like an ox.
> The infant will play near the hole of the cobra,
> And the young child will put his hand into the viper's nest.
> They will neither harm nor destroy
> On all my holy mountain,
> For the earth will be filled with the knowledge of the Lord,
> As the waters cover the sea. (Isa. 11.6-9)

If God exists as the omnibenevolent, all-powerful, creator God depicted in the Abrahamic traditions, it makes sense for God to set the world to rights – to provide the opportunity for the ultimate redemption of all sentient beings. This may be accomplished by bringing them into a flourishing state in a life beyond death where they will receive what was unavailable to them in this life – fulfilment of their natures. Envisioning such a heavenly existence may be beyond human comprehension. Shakespeare was probably right: 'There are more things in heaven and earth ... than are dreamt of in your philosophy' (Hamlet, scene v). Why not? If God does exist, isn't it reasonable to expect a comprehensive eschatology – one that far surpasses human imagination in goodness, beauty and grandeur?

Concluding reflections

What I've attempted to demonstrate in this chapter is that the theist has at her disposal a variety of ways of explaining how it might be that a good and all-powerful God created a world in which there is evil, including pain and suffering, in the natural world. We examined two classical theodicies: free will and soul-making. Each of them has powerful elements necessary for making sense of the evil in the world, but neither of them addresses well a fundamental type of natural evil: the pain, suffering and death intrinsic to biological evolution. Building on the notion of free will and soul-making, the skeleton of a theodicy of fulfilment was put forth utilizing four basic principles. If one begins with the presumption of atheism, then some of these principles will doubtless seem preposterous. But if one begins with the presumption of theism and biological evolution, then it seems to me that something like these four principles is likely true. Our options are limited. This is not to say, of course, that such an account removes the agony or horror of any particular evil or set of evils experienced by human beings or non-human animals. Nor does it mean that every particular case of evil will make sense. But it does set the occasions of evil in a theistic context in which we can perhaps begin to make sense of our complex world. As philosopher Eleonore Stump clarifies:

> [The] project of theodicy is different from the project of explaining the suffering of any particular person. In this respect, theodicy resembles clinical psychology or embryology or any other body of knowledge in which the possession of a general theory is not the same as the ability to apply that theory in any given particular case. Why this person should have become sick in this way, given her genetics and environment, may be mysterious to us, not because we lack the relevant theory, but because the information about this particular person that is necessary in order to apply the general theory to her case is lacking to us. Analogously, it is possible to have a general theory about the justification for God's allowing human suffering in general without being able to understand why any given person suffered as he did. Theodicy is therefore not the project of proposing to explain God's particular reasons for his dealings with any particular person or group of persons.[8]

Yes, there is evil in the world. And yes, God was involved in creating the world in which it exists. Free will accounts for much of the evil in the world, but certainly not all of it. Certain forms of evil, including the natural evil we find in the processes of evolution, could well be necessary components of an unfolding world in which finite physical creatures, including moral agents, exist. And some evils may well be gratuitous; they may have no explicit purpose. Nevertheless, if God does exist, in the eschaton reparations will be made available for all the suffering that sentient creatures have experienced. Pain, suffering and death will have been worth it as those in the new creation experience the eternal goodness and bliss which is the desired fulfilment of all sentient life.

So we have here the framework of a theodicy for our day. But this doesn't solve every problem of evil. In fact, there is a glaring issue that must yet be addressed before examining the difficulties other worldviews face given the evil in the world: the elusiveness of God.

Further reading

Burrell, David B. 2008. *Deconstructing Theodicy: Why Job Has Nothing to Say to the Puzzle of Suffering*. Grand Rapids, MI: Brazos Press. (Burrell argues that rather than offering a theodicy – a futile undertaking, in his judgement – the book of Job deconstructs theodicy and presents Job as seeking to speak to God instead.)

Hick, John. 1996/2007. *Evil and the God of Love*. London: Palgrave Macmillan. (The classic soul-making theodicy is presented and defended.)

Southgate, Christopher. 2008. *The Groaning of Creation: God, Evolution, and the Problem of Evil*. Louisville/London: Westminster John Knox Press. (A thoughtful and informative defense of an evolutionary theodicy; I am indebted to Southgate for this insightful work.)

Stump, Eleonore. 2010. *Wandering in Darkness: Narrative and the Problem of Suffering*. Oxford: Clarendon Press. (A magisterial work of contemporary philosophy dealing with evil and suffering from the perspective of Christian narrative.)

Swinburne, Richard. 1998. *Providence and the Problem of Evil*. Oxford: Clarendon Press. (A recent and powerful defense of the free will theodicy.)

Ward, Keith. 2007. *Divine Action: Examining God's Role in an Open and Emergent Universe*. Philadelphia/London: Templeton Foundation Press. (An insightful and provocative work on divine action.)

CHAPTER FOUR

Divine hiddenness

We have so far examined defenses and theodicies as ways of dealing with the challenge of theistic belief, given the reality of moral and natural evil. Another dimension of the problem of evil has to do with what is sometimes referred to as 'divine hiddenness'. The problem can be characterized in the following way. God's existence is not an obvious feature of the universe. God cannot be seen or heard or touched or experienced by any of the five senses; there is inconclusive evidence for the reality of God. But if God does exist, his existence should be an obvious feature of the universe. Theists, then, carry the burden of providing a reasonable account of why God's existence is not readily apparent. To put it another way, why would God's presence, if God does exist, not be obvious to any and every person seeking to know or know about God? Why would a loving, caring divine being hide from the very creatures God created with the express purpose of having a relationship with him? The absence of reasonable answers to such questions may even provide evidence that there is no divine reality. We could put the problem more concisely this way: either God can't make his presence known or won't do so. If God can't make his presence known, God must not be omnipotent. If God won't make his presence known, God must not be good and loving. But lacking either of these attributes means that God, if God exists, is not the divine being of traditional theism. The other option, of course, is that God does not exist at all.

The issue of divine hiddenness has not only been raised by atheists and agnostics; indeed, theists often concede the difficulty as well. The Hebrew Bible, for example, is filled with references to God's hiding:

'Why do you hide your face, and count me as your enemy?' (Job 13.24)

'Why, O Lord, do you stand far off? Why do you hide yourself in times of trouble?' (Psalm 10.1)

'Rouse yourself! Why do you sleep, O Lord? Awake, do not cast us off forever! Why do you hide your face? Why do you forget our affliction and oppression?' (Psalm 44.23-24)

'Truly you are a God who hides himself, O God of Israel, the Saviour.' (Isaiah 45.15)

The silence of God is related to divine hiddenness, for this too poses a problem for the theist, especially in times of trouble or distress. In Shusaku Endo's novel *Silence*, a young Jesuit priest from Portugal named Sebastian Rodrigues is sent to Japan to comfort Christian converts and to investigate claims that his spiritual mentor has committed apostasy. Out of suspicion and concern about the rapid growth of the Christian faith in Japan, feudal lords, under the auspices of the shogun (chief military commander), attempt to drive Christianity out of Japan by brutally torturing Christians to the point that they either deny their faith or suffer fatal consequences. The novel's plot focuses on a small group of Portuguese priests whose faith is challenged in ways that only the pain and suffering of persecution can achieve. Sebastian describes one particularly horrifying scenario in which a Japanese man named Kichijiro – an apostate who had witnessed the murder of his family before himself recanting – describes his problem with God:

> I do not believe that God has given us this trial to no purpose. I know that the day will come when we will clearly understand why this persecution with all its sufferings has been bestowed upon us – for everything that Our Lord does is for our good. And yet, even as I write these words I feel the oppressive weight in my heart of those last stammering words of Kichijiro on the morning of his departure: 'Why has Deus Sama [God] imposed this suffering upon us?' And then the resentment in those eyes that turned upon me. 'Father,' he had said, 'what evil have we done?'
>
> I suppose I should simply cast from my mind these meaningless words of the coward; yet why does his plaintive voice pierce my breast with all the pain of a sharp needle? Why has Our Lord

imposed this torture and this persecution on poor Japanese peasants? No, Kichijiro was trying to express something different, something even more sickening. The silence of God. Already twenty years have passed since the persecution broke out; the black soil of Japan has been filled with the lament of so many Christians; the red blood of priests has flowed profusely; the walls of the churches have fallen down; and in the face of this terrible and merciless sacrifice offered up to Him, God has remained silent. This was the problem that lay behind the plaintive question of Kichijiro. (pp. 54–5)

While these words are fictional, *Silence* is a work of historical fiction – one based on the actual oral histories of several Japanese communities in the sixteenth century during which Christian men, women and children were rounded up and required to recant or face some of the most gruesome persecutions imaginable.

Now when it comes to enchanting characters like Santa Claus or the Tooth Fairy, we are not surprised when they don't actually make themselves known – when they neither appear nor speak to us. We are not even surprised when certain non-fictional entities that we do believe exist remain hidden from our senses. Quarks and gluons, for example, are unavailable to empirical observation, and yet most of us don't consider their lack of visible detection to be problematic. The reason, of course, is that they are not the kinds of entities that should, if they do in fact exist, be readily available to such detection or experience. God, on the other hand, is such a being. If God exists and is the unsurpassably loving, wise, caring, personal being described by the monotheistic religions, then it seems reasonable to suppose that God should be readily present to us. God should at least offer objective evidence of his reality, especially when we are in doubt about it and could truly benefit from such knowledge.

An argument for God's non-existence

The atheist philosopher Bertrand Russell was once asked what he would say to God if after his death he had a divine encounter and was asked by God why he hadn't believed during his life. Russell's reply: 'Not enough evidence, God! Not enough evidence!' We might wonder what kind of evidence Russell would have preferred. It seems reasonable enough that one form of evidence Russell would have benefitted from (as would the rest of us) is some sort of objective proof that God is really there. Perhaps even better would be a direct encounter with God as a loving, caring, personal being – especially in times of doubt or distress. But Russell never received such confirming evidence and, so as far as we know, died an atheist.

What are we to make of this problem of divine hiding? Philosopher John Schellenberg has argued that the hiddenness of God provides proof that there is no such being. In the following narrative he lays out the problem, in the form of an analogy, with clarity and verve:

> Imagine yourself in the following situation. You're a child playing hide-and-seek with your mother in the woods at the back of your house. You've been crouching for some time now behind a large oak tree, quite a fine hiding place but not undiscoverable – certainly not for someone as clever as your mother. However, she does not appear. The sun is setting, and it will soon be bedtime, but still no mother. Not only isn't she finding you, but, more disconcerting, you can't hear her anywhere: she's not beating the nearby bushes, making those exaggerated 'looking for you' noises, and talking to you meanwhile as mothers playing this game usually do. Now imagine that you start calling for your mother. Coming out from behind the tree, you yell out her name, over and over again. 'Mooooommmmmm!' But no answer. You look everywhere: through the woods, in the house, down the road. An hour passes, and you are growing hoarse from calling. Is she anywhere around? Would she fail to answer if she were around?
>
> Now let's change the story a little. You're a child with amnesia – apparently because of a blow to the head (which of course you don't remember), your memory goes back only a few days – and you don't even know whether you have a mother. You see other children with their mothers and think it would sure be nice to have one. So you ask everyone you meet and look everywhere you can, but without forwarding your goal in the slightest. You take up the search anew each day, looking diligently, even though the strangers who took you in assure you that your mother must be dead. But to no avail. Is this what we should expect if you really have a mother and she is around, and aware of your search? When in the middle of the night you tentatively call out – 'Mooooommmmmm!' – would she not answer if she were really within earshot?[1]

Certainly, Schellenberg argues, if the mother in these scenarios was really around and simply didn't care to respond to her child, she would not be a good mother. A good parent isn't like that. Good parents do what they can to comfort their children, to be present with them, especially in times of need and distress. They hold them, talk to them, and use various means to communicate their love, care and concern. But when it comes to God and human beings, it seems that God (if God exists) is acting more like this absent, uncaring mother than like a good, loving parent. No doubt there are times when good parents are absent from their children. There may be times when it's appropriate, say, for parents to go out for the evening for an intimate dinner date together – something healthy and beneficial for a flourishing relationship. But we know the difference between appropriate times of absence and inappropriate ones. In fact, most countries have laws which recognize the difference and punish parents who are too absent from their children, calling this 'child neglect'. There also may be times when good parents need to shut themselves away from a child – to be intentionally absent and even silent. For example, when a toddler disobeys his parents, they may put him in a 'time-out' in a separate room, away from everyone else, and tell him to be quiet for a time and not to speak to anyone. Despite a child's ranting tantrum, good parents may take some time and not respond at all. This can be a form of discipline and moral education. But again, we generally know the difference between appropriate times of absence and silence on the one hand and relational neglect on the other. If you love someone, you communicate with them; you spend time with them. God seems to do neither with human beings.

Using these intuitions and the traditional theistic understanding of God, Schellenberg develops several versions of the hiddenness argument for God's non-existence. Perhaps the most persuasive of them focuses on non-belief. If God does exist, then reasonable non-belief would not occur, for surely a perfectly loving God would desire that people believe in God. And if God desires that people so believe, God would work it out so that persons would be in a reasonable position to believe. However, reasonable non-belief does occur. There are persons who do not believe in God, and they are reasonable in doing so. They may have studied the evidence, explored their motives of belief, examined why others who believe do so, and so on. Yet despite all of this, they still do not believe, and they see no good reason to believe.

Furthermore, the argument goes, such non-believing persons may be doing so in a morally innocent manner. Their non-belief is not due to a resistance or opposition to God, a desire that God not exist, a moral repugnance to the very idea of God's existing, or any such thing. They simply do not believe and have no good reason to believe. But a perfectly loving God, it seems, would ensure belief in God by all persons. Since there is reasonable non-belief, then, we have solid evidence that God, as a perfectly loving, caring being, does not exist. We can delineate Schellenberg's argument – what we'll call the Divine Hiddenness Argument – this way:

1. If there is a God, he is perfectly loving.
2. If a perfectly loving God exists, reasonable non-belief does not occur.
3. Reasonable non-belief occurs.
4. No perfectly loving God exists (from 2 and 3).
5. Hence, there is no God (from 1 and 4).[2]

This argument is valid (which means that if the premises are true, then the conclusion logically follows): God does not exist. But are the premises true?

Before tackling this argument, we can perhaps bolster it further by adding the challenge posed by the uneven distribution of belief in God around the world.[3] Why, if God exists, is reasonable non-belief so much more widespread in certain parts of the world than in others? Belief in the God of theism is virtually non-existent in Sri Lanka, large portions of India and China and many countries in Africa, to cite several significant examples. Yet in other parts of the word theism is widespread. Why would a perfectly loving God permit such global unevenness in theistic belief?

Some possible reasons for divine hiddenness

The problem of divine hiddenness is indeed a pernicious difficulty for theists. Some have even argued that the problem of divine hiddenness provides a better atheological argument (argument for atheism) than the more familiar arguments from evil described in Chapter 2. So how might the theist reply? Are there plausible reasons for divine hiding?

One way a theist could reply to the Divine Hiddenness Argument is to deny the first premise that, if there is a God, he is perfectly loving. As noted in Chapter 1, this is not a common move, but it has been made by some theists. These dystheists do believe that God exists, but they also believe that God is less than good – some even claim that God is evil. For example, in her widely acclaimed novel, *Their Eyes Were Watching God*, Zora Neil Hurston reflects this viewpoint: 'All gods who receive homage are cruel. All gods dispense suffering without reason. Otherwise, they would not be worshipped. Through indiscriminate suffering men know fear and fear is the most divine emotion. It is the stones for altars and the beginning of wisdom. Half gods are worshipped in wine and flowers. Real gods require blood.'[4] These sentiments may or may not have been held by Hurston herself, but they do capture the enmity some people feel toward God. Perhaps none have felt more strongly this way than those who suffered through the Nazi concentration camps.[5] For many there, the absence of God was glaring, and the silence of God was deafening.

Another way a theist could reply to the Divine Hiddenness Argument is to deny the third premise that reasonable non-belief occurs. Some theists have, in fact, maintained that any non-belief in God is unreasonable. There is no universally held definition of 'unreasonable', but theists who take this approach typically affirm that every case of unbelief is one in which the person is epistemically culpable for their lack of belief. That is, while they do not believe in God, they should so believe. God has made his existence available in such a way to warrant belief in God. I disagree. I think there are cases of reasonable non-belief, so the rest of the responses to the Divine Hiddenness Argument will presuppose this view.

A third way to respond to the Divine Hiddenness Argument is to challenge premise number two which states that if a perfectly loving God exists, reasonable non-belief does not occur. How so? It may be that those persons who do not believe in God are, for one reason or another, not in a state of mind to believe that God exists. For example, given a person's current attitude toward the notion of God, it could be that if the person were (at least up to this point in time) confronted with the reality of the divine presence, rather than entering into a meaningful relationship with God she would instead shut herself off from God. In this case, it's not that the person has already shut herself off from God, but rather that if she were put in a position of having a belief in God, she would not in fact do so;

she would 'harden her heart' toward God instead. In cases like this, God hides. It's not that God wants to remain hidden or alienated from such individuals, but rather that some people are simply not prepared to believe in God and would in fact be worse off if God didn't remain hidden to them.

Related to this point, in the New Testament book the Gospel of Matthew, the author records the words of Jesus to his disciples regarding why he spoke in parables:

> The reason I speak to them in parables is that 'seeing they do not perceive, and hearing they do not listen, nor do they understand'. With them indeed is fulfilled the prophecy of Isaiah that says: 'You will indeed listen, but never understand, and you will indeed look, but never perceive. For this people's heart has grown dull, and their ears are hard of hearing, and they have shut their eyes; so that they might not look with their eyes, and listen with their ears, and understand with their heart and turn – and I would heal them.' (Matthew 13.13-16)

On one interpretation of this passage, Jesus' reason for speaking in parables was that some people are not in a position to hear about God and the truths and purposes of God in a straightforward manner since they have shut their eyes and closed their ears (perhaps knowingly, freely and culpably; perhaps not). The parables, then, are a means of getting those truths and purposes into human hearts and minds by veiling the message in such a way that it non-threateningly and gradually is revealed to them. This veiling may be due to either intentional (and so culpable) unreceptivity, or unintentional (and so non-culpable) unreceptivity.

There are a number of reasons why a person, even though he is intellectually capable of believing that God exists, may not yet be receptive to such belief. For example, given his prior life experiences, he may have reason to doubt that God – a loving and beneficent being who desires a relationship with him – exists. If he has experienced horrific trauma of one sort or another, say, this could produce psychological, emotional or intellectual barriers to his believing that God exists, or at least believing that a good God exists who loves and desires a relationship with him. So while someone in this case might be intellectually capable of such knowledge, a great amount of healing may need to occur before he could be in an emotional or psychological state such that he could form the proper belief about God or enter into a proper relationship with God.

Furthermore, given a person's education and knowledge base, he or she may have reason to doubt that God (a loving and beneficent being who desires a relationship with the person) exists. If one were trained in a certain school of analytic philosophy in the mid-twentieth century, for example, he or she may have come to believe that the very notion of a personal God is a meaningless concept. If one is intellectually convinced that the notion of a personal God is meaningless, it would be difficult to believe that such a God exists – let alone that God desires to be known by and have a meaningful relationship with him!

Related to these points, Paul Moser has argued that God remains hidden in order to prevent certain persons from coming to know God in an inappropriate and unhelpful manner. In sketching out his argument, Moser makes a distinction between propositional knowledge and filial knowledge. The former is knowledge that God exists. The latter is of a different order and is one in which a person 'humbly, faithfully, and lovingly stands in a child's relationship to God as the righteously gracious Father'.[6] In Moser's account, God's perfect love results in God's bringing about our having both propositional and filial knowledge of God. Filial knowledge is essential for a right relationship with God – one that is good for us. Moser describes it this way:

> Divine hiding, like everything else God does, seeks to advance God's good kingdom by promoting what is good for all concerned. So we must keep divine hiding in the context of God's main desire to have people lovingly know God and thereby to become loving as God is loving ... God desires that people turn, for their own good, to the loving God in filial communion and faithful obedience. God's primary aim is not to hide but rather to include all people in God's family as beloved children under God's fatherly guidance. A loving filial relationship with God is God's main goal for every human. This means that God wants us to love, to treasure, God as our Father, not just to believe that God exists (Deuteronomy 6.5; Mark 12.30; James 2.19). So production of mere reasonable belief that God exists will not meet God's higher aim for us. For our own good, God is after something more profound and more transforming than

simple reasonable belief about God. Mere reasonable belief is no match for personal transformation toward God's loving character.[7]

Divine hiddenness, then, is rooted in divine love.

Another reason why a person may not be in a position to have a relationship with God is that one's free will to choose God could be in jeopardy if he or she were directly confronted with God's presence. If God were not hidden, one would be unduly coerced, or forced, as it were, to believe that God exists. In that case, one could not choose to believe that God exists. This limitation of epistemic freedom may well also affect one's moral freedom, for one would likely do good or abstain from doing evil because of either fear of divine punishment or an egoistic desire for success rather than out of love for God, others and the good. God is not interested in moral slaves, so he has made his existence and presence available to all true seekers, but non-coercively so. God's hiding would, again, be due to God's love and concern for all people, even those who are not yet ready or able to believe. God thus makes himself evident in proportion to a person's readiness to receive him. Blaise Pascal is apt on the point:

> Willing to appear openly to those who seek Him with all their heart, and to be hidden from those who flee from Him with all their heart, [God] so regulates the knowledge of Himself that He has given signs of Himself, visible to those who seek Him, and not to those who seek Him not. There is enough light for those who only desire to see, and enough obscurity for those who have a contrary disposition.[8]

These various responses to the Divine Hiddenness Argument seem to demonstrate that reasonable non-belief could occur even if a perfectly loving God exists, contrary to premise two. So the argument has not demonstrated that God, a perfectly beneficent and loving being, does not exist. But perhaps this should not be all that surprising since disproving the existence of God is no small feat! Even though God remains hidden from many people, then, and the silence of God often looms large, there are a number of reasons why divine hiddenness might be God's common modus operandi. Divine hiddenness, then, may not be a great evil after all. In fact, it could be a great good to a great many people.

Divine hiddenness and experiencing God

God-experiences

Before concluding this chapter, it's important to note that divine hiddenness is certainly not the way all persons experience the world. Indeed, there are sane and intelligent people – and a good number of them – who claim to have experienced God in some significant way. It is really quite surprising to see how many types of religious experiences have been recorded, and how diverse they turn out to be. Different schemas may be offered to classify the various types of religious experience, but here we will explore those experiences that include God as a personal and loving agent since these offer counter-evidence to divine hiddenness and silence. Let's call these 'God-experiences'. Many people have had and recorded God-experiences. The most common ones are dissimilar to human-to-human experiences. In the Hebrew Bible the prophet Elijah has a divine encounter that is characteristic of recorded experiences with God in that God does not speak with booming thunder:

> Then a great and powerful wind tore the mountains apart and shattered the rocks before the Lord, but the Lord was not in the wind. After the wind there was an earthquake, but the Lord was not in the earthquake.[12] After the earthquake came a fire, but the Lord was not in the fire. And after the fire came a gentle whisper. (I Kings 19.11-13; NIV)

No audible voice, no visible manifestation, no fanfare; it is a still, small voice – a gentle whisper – speaking in the depths of one's soul that is how most people describe their experiences with God. While one may wish that God would make his presence known in ways more amenable to common human experience, theists argue God has chosen differently. The Spanish mystic and Carmelite nun, Saint Teresa of Avila (1515–82), for example, describes a related experience this way:

> I was at prayer on a festival of the glorious Saint Peter when I saw Christ at my side – or, to put it better, I was conscious of Him, for neither with the eyes of the body nor with those of the soul did I see anything. I thought He was quite close to me and I saw that it was He Who, as I thought, was speaking to me.[9]

Another point worth noting, though, is that not all God-experiences are in the form of a still small voice; some of them have been described as being quite arresting and vivid. In his classic work on religious experience, William James documents many such God-experiences from across the religious traditions, including the following by a clergyman:

> I remember the night, and almost the very spot on the hill-top, where my soul opened out, as it were, into the Infinite, and there was a rushing together of the two worlds, the inner and the outer. It was deep calling unto deep, the deep that my own struggle had opened up within being answered by the unfathomable deep without, reaching beyond the stars. I stood alone with Him who had made me, and all the beauty of the world, and love, and sorrow, and even temptation. I did not seek Him, but felt the perfect unison of my spirit with His. The ordinary sense of things around me faded. For the moment nothing but an ineffable joy and exaltation remained. It is impossible fully to describe the experience. It was like the effect of some great orchestra when all the separate notes have melted into one swelling harmony that leaves the listener conscious of nothing save that his soul is being wafted upwards, and almost bursting with its own emotion. The perfect stillness of the night was thrilled by a more solemn silence. The darkness held a presence that was all the more felt because it was not seen. I could not any more have doubted that He was there than that I was. Indeed, I felt myself to be, if possible, the less real of the two.[10]

Similarly, the following was described by an eminent Islamic convert:

> Allah attracted me to His light with irresistible strength, and I gladly yielded to Him. Everything seemed clear now, everything made sense to me, and I began to understand myself, the Universe and Allah. I was bitterly aware that I had been deceived by my dearest teachers, and that their words were only cruel lies, whether they were aware of it or not. My whole world was shattered in one instant; all concepts had to be revised. But the bitterness in my heart was amply superseded by the ineffable joy of having found my Lord at last, and I was

filled with love and gratitude to Him. I still humbly praise and bless Him for His Mercy with me; without His help, I would have remained in darkness and stupidity forever.[11]

James includes numerous examples of such experiences from across the religious spectrum. And countless books and websites are now available which are devoted to documenting God-experiences and other types of religious experience. It seems that divine encounters are not as uncommon as one might suppose.

Challenges to God-experiences

There have been innumerable experiences of God reported in detail by religious adherents across cultures and throughout history. Some philosophers have argued that given the widespread occurrence of such experiences, an argument for the existence of God can be culled from them. Hindu philosopher Sarvepalli Radhakrishnan writes that 'The possibility of the experience [of God] constitutes the most conclusive proof of the reality of God.'[12] At first blush, such experiences do seem to provide solid evidence for God. After all, surely the many God-experiences that have occurred are not all false or delusory. Or are they? There are various arguments claiming that even if there are significant numbers of God-experiences, this does not constitute evidence for the reality of God.

One argument against the claim that God-experiences provide evidence for God is that such experiences are not verifiable as are other kinds of experiences. Compare a religious experience, sensing the presence of God, with a perceptual experience: seeing a Rose-Breasted Grosbeak (a bird indigenous to my area). If someone claims to see a Rose-Breasted Grosbeak in their backyard, it's easy enough to confirm. Other perceptions can be used to verify whether the claim is true or not – other observers can see it, take pictures of it, or perhaps even catch it. But what about the claim of someone to have had a religious experience? How can this sort of claim be verified? Certainly not in the same way as the bird experience. What other kind of verification might be offered?[13]

In philosophy a distinction is sometimes made between first-person psychological reports, such as 'I seem to see a Rose-Breasted Grosbeak,' and perceptual experiences, such as 'I see a Rose-Breasted

Grosbeak.' With the latter kind of experiences a person can be mistaken. I thought it was a Rose-Breasted Grosbeak, but it turned out to be a Downy Woodpecker (I actually made this mistake one day). With the former kind of experience a person cannot be mistaken. Even though it turned out to be a Downy Woodpecker, the claim that 'I seem to see a Rose-Breasted Grosbeak' is nonetheless true. I did seem to see one. These sorts of first-person, private reports are about the goings on of one's own mind and are referred to as incorrigible experiences; while I might be mistaken about what I see, I cannot be mistaken that I seem to see what I do.

The question then becomes whether religious experiences are corrigible or incorrigible. If they are corrigible, they may well be mistaken. If they are incorrigible, then the experiencer cannot be mistaken about them. However, in that case they are subjective private experiences and so do not provide objective evidence or justification for their being about a reality outside the mind of the one having them. Whether religious experiences are corrigible or incorrigible is a matter of continued philosophical debate.

Another argument against the claim that God-experiences provide justification for believing that God exists is that there are scientific explanations for religious experience. According to Sigmund Freud (1856–1939), certain desires for protection and care are satisfied through the illusion of divine Providence. Freud argued that feelings of helplessness and fear in childhood foster a desire for fatherly, loving protection. This desire, or wish, for a protective individual continues on into adulthood and demands a greater, more powerful being than a human father. This desire, combined with desires for universal justice and a continuation of our own existence after death, is satisfied through the formation of the illusion of divine Providence: a person projects the existence of a God. So God-experiences can be explained as psychological projections which fulfil certain fundamental human needs and longings. There is, then, no evidence from such experiences that God was actually involved in them or that God truly exists.

But perhaps this conclusion is too quick, for even if one has a God-experience which is caused by certain needs and desires, so what? That does not discount the experience or the content of the experience. Suppose that one believes in the existence of a personal and powerful God because of a deep-seated need for a heavenly Father. That does not prove that a personal and powerful God does not exist, nor does it prove that God does not show up in one's experiences. It could be, for example, that God utilizes the notion of familial relationship as a pedagogical tool for teaching people about who God is and to prepare them for experiencing him. In fact, this is precisely what many Jews, Christians and Muslims actually believe and how they interpret passages in their sacred scriptures which refer to God as Father.

More recently, neuroscientific advancements have demonstrated that human minds may have natural affinities for religion, and that religious experience may be the result of neurophysiological causes. Some researchers have concluded, therefore, that religious experiences are ultimately false or delusory – that belief in God and experiences of God are mere tricks played on us by our minds. But this conclusion is unwarranted, for even if it can be shown that there are neurophysiological explanations for religious belief and experiences, it does not follow that they are false or delusory. Most theists historically have held that scientifically adequate explanations can be offered for most natural events. But they also believe that these events are grounded in the causal actions of God. For example, many theists believe that the evolution of living organisms can be described in scientific language, but that this does not eliminate the role of God in guiding the process and sustaining each and every element of it. So even given a scientific explanation of God-experiences and beliefs, this would not prove that God isn't their ultimate cause, nor would it demonstrate that a natural explanation is sufficient.

We will not delve further into the question of whether religious experience provides evidence for God. But it may well be that God is not so terribly elusive after all – especially if we are open to being transformed by a divine encounter.

Further reading

Drange, Theodore. 1998. *Nonbelief and Evil: Two Arguments for the Nonexistence of God*. New York: Prometheus Books. (A nontheist presents arguments against belief in God, including an emphasis on divine hiddenness.)

Howard-Snyder, Daniel and Paul Moser, eds. 2002. *Divine Hiddenness: New Essays*. Cambridge: Cambridge University Press. (A scholarly collection of essays by theists and nontheists.)

James, William. 1916. *The Varieties of Religious Experience: A Study in Human Nature*. New York: Longmans, Green. [Originally published in 1902, A classic work on religious experience, including God-experiences.]

Moser, Paul. 2008. *The Elusive God: Reorienting Religious Epistemology*. Cambridge: Cambridge University Press. (Advanced. For a very accessible presentation of some of the main themes in this book, see Moser's *Why Isn't God More Obvious?* Atlanta, GA: RZIM, 2000.)

Schellenberg, John. 1993. *Divine Hiddenness and Human Reason*. Ithaca, NY: Cornell UP. (Examines various attempts by theists to deal with divine hiddenness and argues that they fall short of rebutting the arguments he presents.)

CHAPTER FIVE

Evil, atheism and the problem of good

As we have seen, the reality of evil poses a serious problem, or rather set of problems, for those who believe in a good, wise and an all-powerful deity. The theist does, it seems, bear the burden of making sense of evil in a world that was created by God for, on the theistic view, this is God's world; God designed, created and sustains it. So why is this world so deeply flawed? The previous two chapters explored attempts at making sense of this. But it is also the case that non-theists face challenges, given the evil that exists in the world. There are a variety of non-theistic worldviews, and in the next chapter we will explore Buddhist and Hindu accounts of evil. In this chapter, we examine some problems confronting the view contrary to theism: atheism.

Problems of evil and the problem of good

At first glance, it may seem that those who deny the existence of God are immune to theoretical problems raised by evil, maintaining that evil is simply inherent to the natural world. While theist and atheist can agree that catastrophe, suffering and nefariousness in all their odious manifestations are matters to oppose whenever and wherever possible, it seems that it is the theist who has her back against the wall given their occurrences, for she is the one who affirms the existence of a divine being who could, and indeed should, eliminate such evils. Nevertheless, evil persists. The atheist, in not believing in the existence of a perfect, divine being, appears to have nothing to explain with respect to evil. The world is just the way the world is, period.

Further reflection, however, reveals that matters may not be so straightforward after all. Sure, disaster, pain and suffering are features of the natural world. But are they in fact evil? As we saw in Chapter 1, there is a moral dimension to evil, just as there is a moral dimension to good. To speak of disaster, suffering and pain as evil is to make a moral claim about them; it is to claim that such things are wrong and should not be the case. The various connections between the good and right and the evil and wrong are complex, to be sure, and we won't tackle all of them here. But important questions worth exploring in this chapter are the following: What exactly is evil on an atheistic view of the world, and why is it so? Is there an objective reality to evil, or is it merely subjective? And how are we to distinguish between good and evil on an atheistic account? Furthermore, when atheists claim that evil provides evidence against the existence of God, to what standard of goodness are they subscribing in making this judgement?

The various problems atheists face can perhaps best be brought to light by considering a true but very disturbing example. Some years ago serial killer Ted Bundy, who confessed to murdering over 30 women, was interviewed about his gruesome proclivities. Here are the frightening words he offered to one of his victims as he later articulated them:

> Then I learned that all moral judgments are 'value judgments', that all value judgments are subjective, and that none can be proved to be either 'right' or 'wrong' ... I discovered that to become truly free, truly unfettered, I had to become truly uninhibited. And I quickly discovered that the greatest obstacle to my freedom, the greatest block and limitation to it, consists in the insupportable 'value judgment' that I was bound to respect the rights of others. I asked myself, who were these 'others"?

Other human beings, with human rights? Why is it more wrong to kill a human animal than any other animal, a pig or a sheep or a steer? Is your life more to you than a hog's life to a hog? Why should I be willing to sacrifice my pleasure more for the one than for the other? Surely, you would not, in this age of scientific enlightenment, declare that God or nature has marked some pleasures as 'moral' or 'good' and others as 'immoral' or 'bad'? In any case, let me assure you, my dear young lady, that there is absolutely no comparison between the pleasure I might take in eating ham and the pleasure I anticipate in raping and murdering you. That is the honest conclusion to which my education has led me – after the most conscientious examination of my spontaneous and uninhibited self.[1]

Let me be clear that in using this example I am not implying that atheists are Ted Bundy-like in any sense (atheists are just as horrified by such evils as everyone else). However, an important question emerges when reflecting on Bundy's words: on what moral grounds can the atheist provide a reasonable response to Bundy's position as he articulates it? The options are limited. If good and evil, right and wrong, have nothing to do with God, as atheists suppose, what *do* they have to do with? There are a number of replies that can be offered from an atheistic perspective.

One moral position an atheist can affirm is moral relativism, either personal or cultural. For the personal moral relativist, morality is an individual matter: you decide for yourself what is right and wrong, good and evil. Morality is in the eye of the beholder. Problems with this view, however, are widely recognized and multifarious. For one, interpersonal critique or criticism would be ruled out by definition. A personal moral relativist could never meaningfully tell someone else they are wrong, for on this view everyone decides for themselves what is right and wrong. You could never say that what someone else was doing was good or evil, for they determine what is good and what is evil.

What could one say to Bundy on this view? Not much, other than something such as 'I don't like what you believe and what you do; it offends me how you brutalize women.' For the personal relativist, though, what difference does it make if someone else is offended by his or her beliefs or actions? When my morality clashes with your morality, there is no ultimate arbiter or standard other than perhaps that the stronger of us forces the other to agree. But this sort of 'might makes right' ethic has horrific consequences, and one need only be reminded of the Nazi reign of terror to see such power morality in full bloom.

What about cultural moral relativism – the view that moral values are the constructions of culture or society? At first glance, grounding morality in culture seems to be an improvement over individual relativism. Indeed, since at least some moral values do vary from culture to culture, this view appears to reflect the way morality actually works. Consider these two examples: the Eskimos see nothing wrong with infanticide, whereas many other North Americans believe infanticide is immoral; the Greeks believed it was wrong to eat the dead, whereas the Callatians believed it was right to eat the dead.[2] Many other examples could be cited as well. So, the cultural relativist claims, morals are simply cultural inventions.

On deeper reflection, though, the problems with cultural relativism are just as challenging as those with individual relativism. One problem is that if good and evil are cultural inventions, then it would always be wrong for someone within that culture to speak out against the moral norms of that culture. If good and evil are defined by culture, then how can good and evil ever be challenged within culture? All moral reformers – Wilberforce, Martin Luther King, Jr, Jesus or Gandhi, for example – would be wrong in challenging the moral norms of their respective cultures. Furthermore, it would be inappropriate for one culture to criticize the actions of another culture; it would have been wrong for the British in 1940s to criticize the genocidal actions of the Nazis; it would be wrong for North Americans today to criticize earlier Americans for owning slaves and so on. Most atheists writing books on evil and morality today reject moral relativism – both individual and cultural. Leading atheist Sam Harris, for example, offers a number of arguments against it. In a manner reminiscent of C. S. Lewis, Harris argues that relativism is self-refuting:

> Moral relativism ... tends to be self-contradictory. Relativists may say that moral truths exist only relative to a specific cultural framework – but, *this* claim about the status of moral truth purports to be true across all possible frameworks. In practice, relativism almost always amounts to the claim that we should be tolerant of moral difference because no moral truth can

supersede any other. And yet this commitment to tolerance is not put forward as simply one relative preference among others deemed equally valid. Rather, tolerance is held to be more in line with the (universal) truth about morality than intolerance is. (*The Moral Landscape*, p. 45, italics in original)

In order to complain about evil within a culture, Harris and other atheists have argued, there needs to be some standard that transcends culture by which to make such a complaint. Cultural relativism provides no such standard.

Another option open to the atheist is that offered by Friedrich Nietzsche. Nietzsche's writings are terse and dense, and his writing style both evocative and elusive. At times it is difficult to know for sure whether you've actually understood him. I suspect that is intentional. But several features of his views are, I think, fairly clear. Nietzsche is perhaps best known for his claim that 'God is dead', killed by human beings. Now that we have killed God – killed the belief that God is really there, that is – we need to move beyond the language of good and evil. Such language had its part to play in the unfolding drama of early human development, but its time has now past. Good and evil as traditionally understood are no longer useful and must be jettisoned. For Nietzsche, moral language is just that: language. Words do not correspond to metaphysical realities. Words are just words. Language does provide a certain order to the world, but the language of good and evil needs to be replaced with a new language – one that does not carry the metaphysical and theological baggage of earlier times.

Nietzsche understood nature to be a struggle for survival. In his book *Beyond Good and Evil*, he criticizes an objective, universal morality that applies to humanity as a whole and argues for different kinds of moralities – each of which applies to different contexts. One type of morality is more appropriate for those who are in a dominant role in society – those who are stronger, healthier, more powerful. Another type of morality is best suited for those in more subordinate roles – those who are weaker, sickly, less able to lead and control. Nietzsche challenges the widely held moral idea that destruction, exploitation and domination are morally objectionable behaviours in every case. In fact, he maintains that living beings desire to demonstrate their strength and manifest their 'will to power'.

What is strong wins. That is the universal law. To speak of right and wrong per se makes no sense at all. No act of violence, rape, exploitation, destruction, is intrinsically 'unjust', since life itself is violent, rapacious, exploitative and destructive and cannot be conceived otherwise.[3]

Most of us would agree, I think, that Nietzsche's view of morality as will to power, with its domination and exploitation of others, seems just as problematic and troubling as moral relativism. It is elitist to the extreme in which the 'superior' individuals cooperate in their struggle against the 'plebians' (the great masses of humanity). This view seems more brutish and potentially cruel than any 'moral theory' I can imagine! In fact, Bundy's statements to the terrified woman he was about to rape seem quite congruent with Nietzsche's moral understanding.

A third approach some atheists have taken is to ground morality (good and evil, right and wrong) in biological evolution. This is the approach of evolutionary biologist Richard Dawkins. In *The Selfish Gene*, he states that 'we are survival machines – robot vehicles blindly programmed to preserve the selfish molecules known as genes'.[4] Morality is not objective in this account, and may even seem to be meaningless. Dawkins claims elsewhere: 'In a universe of blind physical forces and genetic replication, some people are going to get hurt, other people are going to get lucky, and you won't find any rhyme or reason in it, nor any justice. The universe we observe has precisely the properties we should expect if there is, at the bottom, no design, no purpose, no evil and no good, nothing but blind, pitiless indifference. DNA neither knows nor cares. DNA just is.'[5] For Dawkins, our moral beliefs are predetermined posits of our genetic machinery, selfishly programmed to advance the gene pool. He grants that selfishness does not at first glance appear to offer a solid foundation for a moral theory. But further reflection leads to the conclusion that it does. Morality is an evolutionary mechanism for gene replication.

In his more recent book, *The God Delusion*, Dawkins clarifies and expounds on his position. He affirms that an obvious way in which genes ensure their own survival is by programming individual organisms to be selfish. However, he argues, sometimes genes influence organisms to act altruistically in order to ensure their own selfish survival. This happens most commonly with an organism's close kin: brothers and sisters and children. The reason for this, he says, is that when genes programme particular organisms to favour their own genetic family, they are more likely to advance copies of themselves.

Besides genetic kinship, another factor that is important in Dawkins's moral account is what he calls 'reciprocal altruism'. This occurs not only with close relatives, but among various members of the species and even outside the species. This is the 'you scratch my back and I'll scratch yours' idea, and it is not uncommon among members of the animal kingdom. For example, in the bird population where there exist harmful parasites, birds perform mutual grooming techniques on fellow birds to remove the parasites since they have no limbs to remove them themselves. With certain bird populations, there are three types of birds which Dawkins labels 'Suckers', 'Cheaters' and 'Grudgers'. Suckers are those birds that groom any other bird; Cheaters are those birds that refuse to groom another bird unless it presents itself to be groomed; and Grudgers are the ones that groom only those who reciprocate in grooming them. Grudgers groom other Grudgers and Suckers, but they will not groom Cheaters. Of the three types, the Grudgers are the ones that flourish, demonstrating the evolutionary value of reciprocal altruism.

There are two additional elements to Dawkins's moral account. The first is a reputation for generosity in which an organism acts altruistically so that others will form the belief that it is generous. Especially in human society, where language and gossip are involved, one's reputation is significant. If one has a reputation for cheating and stealing and lying, he or she will not generally have the same survival value as someone else with a reputation of being moral: kind, generous and altruistic. So your gene pool is more effectively advanced when others believe that you are moral.

The next element is buying authentic advertising, the notion that an organism acts morally in order to prove that he has more than another, that he is dominant and superior and so capable of acting altruistically. Only a superior individual can afford to be generous, and by making one's altruistic activities known, the individual demonstrates to others one's superiority and dominance. Dawkins offers an example of this principle in nature with the Arabian babblers, little birds that live in social groups. Dominant birds in the group assert their superiority by feeding subordinates, and they compete for the role of sentinel, risking their own lives by sitting on a high branch and warning others eating on the ground of impending dangers. Their reason for doing so is the express purpose of demonstrating their superiority and thus attracting mates.

So we have the four major components of Dawkins's attempt to provide a justification for acting morally and for having moral beliefs:

a. genetic kinship: helping one's family members, even at one's own expense;
b. reciprocation: beyond one's kin, the repayment of favours given where both sides benefit from the transaction;
c. acquiring a reputation for generosity and kindness: convincing others that one is moral;
d. buying authentic advertising: strutting one's good deeds before others to impress them, demonstrate one's superiority, and thus secure a mate.

We can summarize Dawkins's position this way: our genes are preprogrammed to selfishly replicate themselves. Nevertheless, individual organisms don't always act selfishly; they also act altruistically and morally as this offers better gene propagation over the long term. It appears that naturalistic evolution has provided us with four fundamental principles for being moral.

An obvious problem with Dawkins's view, however, is that all of this seems to have little to do with what we generally understand to be morality – with objective good and evil, right and wrong. On this account, a person is kind to his neighbour, rather than raping her, because he's been preprogrammed by his genes to do so (at least most individuals have been so preprogrammed), and he's been so programmed only because acting this way confers evolutionary advantage on the organism. There is no objective good and evil here; there is no real right and wrong. We simply call certain things 'evil' and others 'good' because our genes have, through eons of evolutionary struggle, advanced by our believing this way. But do atheists who affirm this view of morality really believe that rape, murder and the like are evil only in the sense that they have become socially taboo for purposes of evolutionary advantage? Would this be a reasonable response to Bundy?

A fourth approach to an atheistic account of morality has been put forth by evolutionary ethicist and atheist philosopher of science

Michael Ruse and his colleague Edward O. Wilson. They agree with Dawkins that morality is rooted in evolution, but they disagree with his conclusion that there are therefore principles by which to ground objective morality:

> Morality, or more strictly our belief in morality, is merely an adaptation put in place to further our reproductive ends. Hence the basis of ethics does not lie in God's will – or in the metaphorical roots of evolution or any other part of the framework of the Universe. In an important sense, ethics as we understand it is an illusion fobbed off on us by our genes to get us to cooperate. It is without external grounding. Ethics is produced by evolution but is not justified by it because, like Macbeth's dagger, it serves a powerful purpose without existing in substance ... Unlike Macbeth's dagger, ethics is a shared illusion of the human race.[6]

So while most people believe that moral values are objectively real, it turns out that they are not. They are merely illusions foisted on us through evolution so that our species continues to flourish and advance. Ruse and Wilson do not in any way attempt to defend or smuggle in an objective morality; good and evil are not real. This is a bold claim, and they should be commended for their unfrivolous consistency and willingness to follow their position to its logical conclusion, as hard as it may be to affirm. In their view, we and our beliefs are simply the byproducts of a 'nature red in tooth and claw'. Good and evil are illusory.

The *Edinburgh Review*, a highly respected British magazine of the nineteenth century, observed that if people come to believe that morality is based on a naturalistic version of evolution, 'most earnest-minded men will be compelled to give up these motives by which they have attempted to live noble and virtuous lives, as founded on a mistake; our moral sense will turn out to be a mere developed instinct.... If these views be true, a revolution in thought is imminent, which will shake society to its very foundations by destroying the sanctity of conscience and the religious sense.'[7] This may be overstating the case. But again, in the view of morality espoused by Ruse and Wilson, what could we say to Bundy? This view of right and wrong does not appear to provide a satisfactory account of morality – neither one that squares with what we know about good and evil (rape and murder are really wrong, whether

Bundy agrees or not), nor one that provides a foundation for living the moral life that most of us would affirm.

A fifth approach an atheist might take in accounting for good and evil is utilitarianism. This is the view that morally right actions are those that produce the most good, 'good' typically defined in terms of happiness or pleasure: the greatest happiness (or pleasure) for the greatest number. One recent version of utilitarianism has been articulated and defended by atheist Sam Harris. Harris argues that science can determine moral values, and that morality is grounded in consciousness and human well-being. That which is morally bad should be understood as the worst possible misery. Moral good, then, at a bare minimum, is to avoid the worst possible misery for every conscious being. This is a form of utilitarianism in which happiness or pleasure is replaced with well-being.

Utilitarianism as a moral theory has some virtues. For one, it is an objective system, rather than a relative one, and it provides an answer, an action-guiding principle, for every moral situation: act in a way that promotes the most happiness (or pleasure or well-being). It also seems to get to the very heart of morality: alleviating human suffering and promoting flourishing. But utilitarianism also raises moral conundrums, some of which are quite problematic. One obvious problem is this: how would we quantify, scientifically or otherwise, the happiness or well-being of a particular action when the consequences that follow from that action may well be virtually endless? And how would we measure, scientifically or otherwise, differences between various sorts of happiness or well-being?

Additional problems loom. Suppose, for example, that we are weighing two actions, and each of them results in ten units of happiness or well-being (measuring such things no doubt raises challenges of its own!). The only difference between them is that one of the actions involves our telling the truth and the other one telling a lie. In utilitarianism, the actions would be morally equivalent, since they would both bring about equal units of happiness. If truth is a good thing, which most of us take it to be, then the principles of utilitarianism have led us to an unacceptable moral conclusion: lying is morally equivalent to telling the truth. Another objection is even more disturbing. Suppose there is a utilitarian surgeon caring for three patients. One patient needs a liver transplant, one needs a heart, and the third needs two lungs. Fortuitously, a homeless man wanders into the clinic. After an examination, the surgeon determines that this man is in good health. So, using the principles of utilitarianism, he concludes that by sacrificing him (removing his organs which will, undoubtedly, cause him to die), there will be more moral good accomplished – more happiness or well-being for more people. This conclusion of the 'morally good' thing to do – taking the life of an innocent person for the well-being of several others – offends our moral sensibilities. Indeed, it seems horribly wrong.

Back to Bundy. Deciding whether it is good or evil, right or wrong, to rape and kill someone based on how much overall happiness follows from the act seems a very strange way to make moral decision. I would say it makes an appalling one. Perhaps some version of utilitarianism can be developed to overcome these difficulties. If not, it seems doomed as a viable moral theory.

The problem of good and the moral argument for God

So far we have been focusing on evil and the problem atheists face given its reality. But just as there is a problem of evil for atheists, so too there is a problem of good – a problem with affirming the reality of objective good in a world in which there is no transcendent and beneficent deity. Atheists and theists can agree that we have capacities for understanding fundamental moral truths, just as we have capacities for grasping mathematical or geometrical truths. We can know that treating homeless children with compassion is good, just as we can know that torturing babies for fun is evil. We are able to recognize virtues such as kindness, selflessness, mercy and love, just as we are able to recognize vices such as selfishness, slander and prejudice. And we are able to distinguish between good persons, such as Mother Teresa and the Dalai Lama, and evil persons, such as Adolf Hitler and Ted Bundy.

In his book *Mere Christianity*, C. S. Lewis argues this point with respect to moral language. In noting that people quarrel and argue, he states that individuals do not merely clash or fight; no, they argue and debate about right and wrong. In doing so, their actions reflect the fact that they believe in objectively real moral principles. If morals were merely subjective feelings or desires, the only thing that would matter would be power. In Nietzschean fashion, the stronger would simply crush the weaker. But what often happens between individuals (and larger groups, including nations) is that we say such things as 'What you are doing is unfair,' or 'You have no right to do what you are doing.' If these were mere emotional utterances, who would care about alleged rights or duties? Making such claims would be like saying 'ouch' when stuck with a pin, or 'I don't like this' when being put upon. Indeed, the language common across cultures and nations includes praise and blame, which would be meaningless if there were no objective moral values. When the toll booth takes my money and the gate fails to open, I do not conclude that it is acting immorally (though I might call it a name or two). The booth is not morally blameworthy as a thief is when he takes my money. We use moral language for persons, and it is meaningful to us. And this meaningful language reflects our moral experiences, which are of an objective sort. This only makes sense, Lewis argued, if moral truths are discovered, not invented, and if we have the capacity to discover them.

Given all this, the question then becomes which view of the world – one with no God or one with God – makes better sense of it. A number of atheists argue that, while there is an objectivity to good and evil, no God is necessary to affirm it. William Rowe, for example, says that 'the claim that God is needed for morality to be objective is absurd'.[8] Daniel Dennett states, 'I have uncovered no evidence to support the claim that people, religious or not, who don't believe in reward in heaven and/or punishment in hell are more likely to kill, rape, rob, or break their promises than people who do.'[9] And Christopher Hitchens comments: 'Name one ethical statement made, or one ethical action performed, by a believer that could not have been uttered or done by a nonbeliever.'[10] One does not need a God to affirm the good or to be good. On this point the evidence seems clear enough. Atheists can be as good (or evil) as theists.

However, to know the good or live according to the good is quite different from justifying or having a foundation or explanation for the good. To affirm a knowledge of objective good and evil without providing an objective justification for good and evil is to affirm a moral epistemology (moral knowledge) without providing a moral ontology (foundational existence of morality) to substantiate it.[11] The question at hand is this: what accounts for objective good and evil in the atheistic view? What makes the atheists' notions of good and evil, right and wrong, more than mere hunches, gut feelings, personal subjective opinions, or illusions emanating from various aspects of biological evolution?

In order to have a consistent and reasonable objective moral stance – a moral stance in which you can substantiate the claim that this is right and that is wrong, this is good and that is evil – you need an objective moral basis. Objective moral values require an objective foundation and explanation, and it seems that none of the atheistic accounts described above provides us with one. We can put the atheist's problem concisely:

> If moral notions such as good and evil exist objectively, then there must be an objective foundation for their existence.
> Atheism offers no objective basis for the existence of moral notions such as good and evil.
> Therefore, for the atheist, moral notions such as good and evil must not objectively exist.

The problem is that most of us really do believe and act as though objective moral values exist. Theists argue that such beliefs make sense if there exists a God – a morally perfect being who transcends the finite physical universe and in whom objective morality is grounded – but they do not make sense if the material universe is the totality of all that exists and human beings emerged from mere valueless, blind physical processes in this universe. For how is it possible for impersonal, valueless, purely natural processes to produce universal, objective moral values? So we can add the further argument:

> If there is no God, no objective moral values, such as good and evil, exist.
> Good and evil do exist as objective moral values.
> Therefore, God exists.

Surprisingly, then, rather than proffering evidence against God, the reality of evil has turned out to provide evidence for the existence of God!

But perhaps we have come to our conclusion too quickly. Do we truly need to posit a God in order to ground objective moral values? As we saw above, some atheists have affirmed that there are objective moral values; that good and evil, right and wrong, transcend individuals and culture, but that their existence does not depend on God's existing. Rather, good and evil are simply fundamental dimensions of reality; there are moral laws that are just as real as physical laws. Philosopher Walter Sinnott-Armstrong holds this view. 'In fact,' he says, 'many atheists are happy to embrace objective moral values. I agree with them. Rape is morally wrong. So is discrimination against gays and lesbians. Even if somebody or some group thinks that these acts are not morally wrong, they still are morally wrong ...' He continues, '[Agreeing that some acts are objectively morally wrong] implies nothing about God, unless objective values depend on God. Why should we believe that they do?'[12] Objective moral values are simply a part of the universe in which we find ourselves.

We might ask what accounts for, or explains, or grounds these objective moral values. Did the big bang event somehow spew forth non-physical values and moral laws? Sinnott-Armstrong offers this explanation: 'What makes rape immoral is that rape harms the victim in terrible ways ... What's immoral about causing serious harms to other people without justification? ... It simply is. Objectively.'[13] Harming victims is bad, he says, so it is morally wrong. Rape is evil because it hurts someone. Nothing further needs to be explained.

We can and should all agree that rape is immoral and harming others is evil, but affirming that something is immoral and evil and having a reasonable justification for its being so are two very different matters. To use a simple example, I could wholeheartedly believe that my automobile will turn on when I turn the key and yet have no understanding of auto mechanics. I could still function well in society, driving from place to place, and never consider what is involved, electrically and electro-mechanically, in the process of the switch causing the engine to turn on. If someone asked me to provide an explanation or justification for the automobile turning on when I turn the key and my reply was simply 'It just does,' that would be no answer at all. The fact of the matter is that the flow of an electric charge through the switch to the starter (among other factors) provides an explanation for the engine turning on. This is what accounts for the fact that when I turn the key the engine starts. To have a real explanation for cases such as this, we need something more than 'it just does'.

Similarly, it can be argued that the same need for explanation applies to good and evil. If one replies to the question of why raping a person is evil by saying that 'it hurts the person', and that the reason hurting someone is evil is because 'it just is', do we really have an explanation? Theists argue that we do not. Atheists such as Sinnott-Armstrong argue that we do – that there are brute givens in our world, and moral values are examples of them. Both atheists and theists end up affirming brute givens (for theists, God is a brute given). I leave it up to you to decide whether this or the other atheist accounts provide a good answer for Bundy.

Concluding reflections

In this chapter, we have seen that the theist is not alone in having problems due to the reality of evil. The atheist does as well. We explored six different ways in which an atheist might provide an accounting for the moral notions of good and evil that we experience: moral relativism, Nietzschean 'might makes right', Dawkins's evolutionary morality, morality as evolutionary illusion, utilitarianism and atheistic moral objectivism. The first five accounts seem to me to miss the mark with respect to how most of us think about morality and the language we use to express what we mean by it. Most of us believe that rape, murder, selfishness and the like are really bad – objectively so, and that kindness, generosity and selfless love are really good – objectively so. If the first five accounts were the only options available to atheism, it seems to me that the atheist would be doomed in her ability to offer a satisfactory account of morality – one that provides a basis for real right and wrong, good and evil.

But the atheist is not necessarily left in a moral bog; there is another game in town. Perhaps there are objective moral values that are simply a part of the universe we inhabit, and their existence does not depend on the reality of a transcendent, morally perfect God. How are we to know? In making this kind of assessment, no amount of scientific research will provide the answer. Like many of the deepest issues humanity has struggled with, we have arrived at the foundational level of philosophical and moral intuitions and reasoning. Here there will be dialogue and disagreement. But one thing is for certain. As with theists, atheists are also not immune to the theoretical difficulties raised by the reality of evil.

Further reading

Baggett, David and Jerry Walls. 2011. *Good God: The Theistic Foundations of Morality*. Oxford: Oxford University Press. (The authors argue that moral notions (right and wrong, good and evil) require God as their foundation.)

Copan, Paul. 2008. 'God, Naturalism, and the Foundations of Morality', in *The Future of Atheism: Alister McGrath and Daniel Dennett in Dialogue*, ed. Robert Stewart. Minneapolis, MN: Fortress Press. (This article, which argues that objective moral values exist and are dependent on God, can also be found online at http://www.paulcopan. com/articles/pdf/God-naturalism-morality.pdf.)

Mitchell, Basil. 1980. *Morality: Religious and Secular*. Oxford: Oxford University Press. (Argues for the importance of religion for the moral life.)

Nietzsche, Friedrich. *Beyond Good and Evil*. Trans. R. J. Hollingdale. New York: Penguin Books, 1973. (The classic work by Nietzsche which rejects the Western notions of truth and God, good and evil.)

Sinnott-Armstrong, Walter. 2009. *Morality Without God*. Oxford: Oxford University Press. (Sinnott-Armstrong argues for the independence of morality from religion.)

Smart, John J. C. and Bernard Williams. 1973. *Utilitarianism: For and Against*. Cambridge: Cambridge University Press. (A famous debate on the issue.)

CHAPTER SIX

Evil and suffering in Hinduism and Buddhism

Problems of evil are typically focused on theists of one stripe or another, and it is commonly assumed that non-theistic religions are devoid of such difficulties. In fact, whatever one's religious tradition, every conscious person has had to deal with the experience of evil in his or her life. Given the ubiquity of evil, pain and suffering, all of the major world religions have addressed the subject. So far, the chapters in this book have focused on debates and issues relevant to theism or atheism. In this chapter, we will examine the ways in which two major non-theistic religions address evil and suffering, Hinduism and Buddhism, for interest in them is becoming increasingly important, and they offer unique and fascinating solutions to the problems.

Karma and rebirth

To begin, it is important to note that within every major religion is a belief about a transcendent reality underlying the natural, physical world. In Western religion,[1] by which I am referring primarily to the three religions of Abrahamic descent, namely Judaism, Christianity and Islam, Ultimate Reality is conceived in terms of a personal divine being. God is personal, God is the creator of all and God is perfect in every respect. Other attributes of God include omniscience, omnipotence and immutability, to name a few. In Eastern religion, and here I am referring primarily to Buddhism and some forms of Hinduism, Ultimate Reality is understood quite differently. It is an absolute state of being rather than a personal, omniscient, omnipotent creator God. It is beyond description via a set of attributes for it is undifferentiated, Absolute Reality. Hindus refer to it as Brahman. For Buddhists, the name varies; Shunyata for example, or Nirvana. These unique conceptions bring with them distinct understandings of other significant issues as well, including evil and suffering.

Furthermore, it seems that Western religious traditions and Eastern – in particular, Indian – religious traditions have different foci when it comes to evil and suffering. As we have seen, the Western traditions are primarily focused on making sense of evil in a world created by God, or justifying the actions, nature or existence of God, given the reality of evil in the world. The major concern is God – God's existence and nature. In the Indian traditions, Hinduism and Buddhism, there is also an attempt to explain the evil, pain and suffering in the world. However, for these traditions, the primary concern is not with God, but with justice, moral law and moral chance. While they seek an explanation for evil, they do not generally seek an accounting of the ways and nature of God (for most Buddhists, for example, there is no God).

Within Hinduism and Buddhism, the doctrines of karma and rebirth developed as an explanation for the problem of evil; or, more specifically, as a way of explaining why there is evil and good, pain and pleasure, misery and happiness. At first glance, it seems that there is no algorithm by which to make sense of the way these different experiences occur. They seem to be random. A tornado swirls through a town, killing some of its inhabitants and sparing others. Two children are born into a loving, caring family; one dies of leukemia as a young child, the other lives into old age. Lightning strikes a tree in a dry forest and a fire ensues; some of the animals escape unscathed, while others burn in agony.

Furthermore, many times good people suffer and wicked people flourish. It's not uncommon for the selfless to be taken advantage of and for the selfish to prosper. It appears that much of morality is up to chance. But this cannot be correct, for in that case there would be no cosmic justice. There is a sense in all of us, or at least many of us, that universal justice does exist. One of the reasons we do the right and avoid the wrong, that we value the good and reject the evil, is because of the belief that there is a connection between our moral actions and the results that follow from them. If we do what's right, there will be reward; if we do what's wrong, there will be punishment. In one way or another, all of the major religious traditions affirm this. So how is this cosmic justice problem to be solved?

The Hindu and Buddhist solution to this problem is that of karma (or kamma in Pali). The term 'karma' has various meanings. It literally means deed or action – what one does. It can also mean one's intention or motivation for a given action, or what happens to an individual. Its broader meaning, sometimes referred to as the 'law of karma', is a law of moral causation, including the results of one's actions. Understood this way, it involves causal connections linking what an individual does to what happens to them. Many people have a sense of this in the way they view the world; it's not unique to Hindus and Buddhists. Many people believe, for example, that what goes around comes around, or that we reap what we sow. It is common among human beings to think that there is comic justice – that goodness is rewarded and evil punished. In Western religions this entails God's governing the universe, including the view (for some theists, that is) that those who are good and forgiven by God are rewarded in heaven and those who are evil and reject the grace of God suffer in hell. For Hindus and Buddhists, karma is the solution.

So how does karma work? There are different sorts of explanations offered by various Hindu and Buddhist thinkers. Karma is a comprehensive causal law in which an individual's actions determine the future situations and experiences of the individual. Fundamental to karma is the claim that universal justice is accomplished in that the good and evil experienced by an individual are not due to chance, but are the result of actions the individual performed in the past – either in this life or in a previous one. Karma preserves the moral law in that if one does what is right and good, there will be reward; if one does what is wrong and evil, there will be punishment. While it seems that justice does not always prevail, for some who do good suffer and some who do evil flourish, nevertheless, it will be accomplished. For even if justice is not meted out in this life, it will be eventually. A person could steal from someone and yet never pay for that action in this life. But he/she will ultimately pay. He may, for example, be reborn to a life in which someone steals from him. The cosmic scales are eventually balanced in every case.

In its popular formulations, rebirth (also referred to as 'reincarnation') is the view that the conscious self transmigrates from one physical body to the next after death. Every human being has lived a former life, perhaps as another human being or perhaps as another kind of organism – an animal or an insect. Those who affirm rebirth and karma often point to a difficulty they see with the Western view of justice and the inequalities experienced in this life: it seems exceedingly unfair that one child is born healthy into a wealthy, loving family, for example, whereas another child is born sickly into a poor, cruel environment. If there is a creator God who brought these two persons into the world, such a God seems to be unloving and unjust. However, if the two children are reaping the consequences of actions they performed in previous lives, this provides a justification for the inequalities. Another reason sometimes given for the belief in rebirth is that many people claim to have experienced a previous life, and sometimes they can even document events which have occurred hundreds or thousands of years prior to their birth.[2] Even the more common *déjà vu* experiences are cited as evidence of having lived a previous life.

In order to get clear on Hindu and Buddhist conceptions of evil and suffering and how karma and rebirth work in these traditions, it will be helpful to first explore their views of Ultimate Reality.

A Hindu conception of Ultimate Reality and evil

Hinduism, whose origins date back more than 5,000 years, is one of the oldest religions of recorded history. It is syncretistic, engulfing many distinct belief systems and worldviews. In fact, there are theistic, pantheistic, panentheistic and polytheistic forms of Hinduism. Given this wide diversity, it is impossible to provide a comprehensive summary of Hindu thought in a book such as this on just about any subject, not the least of which is the matter of evil and suffering. So for our purposes we will home in on one school of Hinduism that is frequently discussed in Western literature on evil and suffering: Advaita Vedānta. This Advaita (non-dualism) school of Hinduism includes the belief that Ultimate Reality, indeed all reality, is divine, or Brahman, and Brahman alone. The eighth-century Indian philosopher Shankara (788–820 CE) provides one of the clearest articulations of this view: 'Brahman is the reality – the one existence, absolutely independent of human thought or idea. Because of the ignorance of our human minds, the universe seems to be composed of diverse forms. It is Brahman alone.'[3]

This is pantheism in that reality is fully divine, and it is monism in that there is only one reality. All apparent distinctive characteristics within Brahman and between Brahman and the world are ultimately illusory. For the Advaitin, this is true of all (apparent) distinctions, between all (apparent) things, even between one's self (Atman) and Brahman. In this version of Hindu thought, Ultimate Reality is understood to be the undifferentiated Absolute.[4] All is one and all is Brahman.

> Just as, my dear, the bees prepare honey by collecting the essences of different trees and reducing them into one essence, and as these (juices) possess no discrimination (so that they might say) 'I am the essence of this tree, I am the essence of that tree,' even so, indeed, my dear, all these creatures though they reach Being do not know that they have reached the Being. Whatever they are in this world, tiger or lion or wolf or boar or worm or fly or gnat or mosquito, that they become. That which is the subtle essence, this whole world has for its self. That is the true. That is the self. That are thou …'[5]

For non-Advaitins, it might be difficult to conceive of the absence of all distinctions, especially between oneself (or apparent self, that is) and all other (apparent) things, including Brahman. From our experiences we tend to infer that we are unique individuals, separate identities from other people, things and Brahman. So a question which naturally arises is: why are we not experiencing this undifferentiated unity with Brahman of which the Advaitin speaks? Why do we believe that we are separate, unique, individual entities and that distinctions are a real dimension of the world? One Advaitin answer is provided by Shankara. As he explains it, there is a distinction between Brahman as 'with' and Brahman as 'without' qualities or attributes. Brahman with attributes is what we find in the Hindu scriptures, and is especially important for meditation purposes. We are first introduced in the scriptures to Brahman as good, and perfect, and blissful, Lord and Creator, and so forth, as this prepares us for the deeper (and more difficult to grasp) notion of the supremely real Brahman as having no attributes.

> Brahman is supreme. He is the reality – the one without a second. He is pure consciousness, free from any taint. He is tranquility itself. He has neither beginning nor end. He does not change. He is joy for ever.
>
> He transcends the appearance of the manifold, created by Maya. He is eternal, for ever beyond reach of pain, not to be divided, not to be measured, without form, without name, undifferentiated, immutable. He shines with His own light. He is everything that can be experienced in this universe.
>
> The illumined seers know Him as the uttermost reality, infinite, absolute, without parts – the pure consciousness. In Him they find that knower, knowledge and known have become one.[6]

The question then is how could Brahman-with-attributes – the perfect Lord and Creator of all – bring about a world with evil in it? Here Shankara utilizes a free-will theodicy, albeit an Eastern version in which karma is central.

> The Lord ... cannot be reproached with inequality of dispensation and cruelty, 'because he is bound by regards'. If the Lord on his own account, without any extraneous regards, produced this unequal creation, he would expose himself to blame; but the fact is, that in creating he is bound by certain regards, i.e., he has to look to merit and demerit [karma]. Hence the circumstance of creation being unequal is due to the merit and the demerit of the living creatures created, and is not a fault for which the Lord it to blame.[7]

In other words, we have created evil through our own choices and actions. Brahman has established a moral order in which karma is a fundamental aspect, but Brahman is not culpable for the evil in it. In some ways, this is quite similar to the Western free-will theodicy we examined in an earlier chapter.

Remember, though, all of this is to be considered within the paradigm of the unenlightened understanding of Brahman-with-attributes. For the truly enlightened, Brahman is without attributes. All is one and undifferentiated. Ultimately, then, there is no difference between good and evil. At the level of the real, even merit and demerit are illusory. Such apparent distinctions are due to maya, spiritual ignorance and illusion. So what brought about this unenlightened state? What initiated maya? If Brahman is fundamental reality – the all, including our own true self – then who or what is responsible for our current state? In Hindu mythology, maya is depicted as a divine goddess, Mahamaya, who deludes us and leads us astray. Many Hindu philosophers interpret maya not as a goddess but rather as the great veiling of the true, Unitary Self. It is unclear what actually originated the veil, and Hindu thinkers have suggested various possibilities. What they virtually all agree on, though, is that the universe it eternal. In that case perhaps there need be no origin for it.

Yet another question naturally arises from this view: how do we overcome this grand illusion? The Advaitin answer is that we need to advance to an enlightened state in order to overcome the veil of cosmic ignorance and so to escape the evil and suffering of the experienced world. We can accomplish this by moving beyond the rational mind, and we do this most effectively through meditation on the deep truths. Shankara clarifies:

'Brahman is neither the gross nor the subtle universe. The apparent world is caused by our imagination, in its ignorance. It is not real. It is like seeing the snake in the rope. It is like a passing dream' – that is how a man should practice spiritual discrimination, and free himself from his consciousness of this objective world. Then let him meditate upon the identity of Brahman and Atman, and so realize the truth …

Give up the false notion that the Atman is this body, this phantom. Meditate upon the truth that the Atman is 'neither gross nor subtle, neither short nor tall', that it is self-existent, free as the sky, beyond the grasp of thought. Purify the heart until you know that 'I am Brahman'. Realize your own Atman, the pure and infinite consciousness.

Just as a clay jar or vessel is understood to be nothing but clay, so this whole universe, born of Brahman, essentially Brahman, is

Brahman only – for there is nothing else but Brahman, nothing beyond That. That is the reality. That is our Atman. Therefore, 'That art Thou' – pure, blissful, supreme Brahman, the one without a second.[8]

By engaging in proper meditation, we can finally escape the illusory power of maya and enter into moksha – the enlightened realization that reality is one, multiplicity is illusion, only the undifferentiated Absolute is real, and pain and suffering are illusory. While moksha is the goal, it is recognized in Advaita Vedanta (indeed in most forms of Hinduism) that true enlightenment will not be achieved immediately. Indeed, it may not be achieved in this life. It may take many rebirths or reincarnations before the power of maya and the negative influences of karma are completely expunged. But it is in this final state, this ultimate enlightenment, that evil and suffering will be understood for what they are: grand illusions brought about through a cosmic veil of ignorance.

A Buddhist conception of Ultimate Reality and suffering

Buddhism emerged from the Hindu tradition in India around the fifth century bce. Ultimate Reality in Buddhism, at least in one major Buddhist school called Madhyamika (the school of the 'Middle Way'), as developed by Nagarjuna, is sunyata, which is translated as 'Emptiness' or 'The Void'. At first glance, it may seem that emptiness and Ultimate Realty are contradictory notions. How can something real be empty? Many Buddhist scholars understand 'being real' as 'being independent of other things'. Buddhist scholar Masao Abe clarifies:

The Buddhists believe that to be called 'substantial or real' a thing must be able to exist on its own. However, if we look at the universe, we find that everything in it exists only in relation to something else. A son is a son only in relation to his father; and a father similarly in relation to his son. Fatherhood does not exist on its own but only in relation to something else. The Buddhists use the word svabhāva to denote existence on its own, that is, nondependent existence, which alone, according to them, qualifies as true or genuine existence. But if everything in the world depends on something else for being what it is, then nothing in the universe can be said to possess svabhāva or genuine existence; hence it is empty.[9]

In this Buddhist view (and indeed in most Buddhist views), there are no substantial entities – things which have independent existence. The Buddha himself understood the world to be one of transiency, and this is because all discernable entities are in fact composite; all is involved in the fluidity of universal change. Such unstable realities cannot be ultimately real. Ultimate Reality is in fact emptiness. There is neither Atman nor Brahman, there is no self but Anatman, or no-self. Every (apparent) thing – planets, mountains, animals, persons and so on – are in reality abstractions of events or processes, events or processes which are dependent on other events or processes. Even though things appear to be stable and substantial, this appearance comes from abstracting the various experiences had and then mentally reifying substantial entities, including the self. But these are merely processes. In fact, all is in flux. In addition, all events and processes originate out of a self-sustaining causal nexus in which each link arises from another, which Buddhists call the doctrine of inter-dependent arising (pratitya-sumutpada). All events and processes are connected to other events and processes. Nothing in the nexus is independent; everything arises from something else.

Karma is one of the causes in the nexus of inter-dependent arising. Because of ignorance (avidya), we continue to experience the effects of karma, and this keeps us within the cycle of cause and effect, death, suffering and rebirth. In order to escape the illusory world of permanence, as Nagarjuna explains it, we need to recognize sunyata, and so come to see that there are no finite or infinite substances – no individual or permanent selves or beings. It is in this enlightened state that we can ultimately break through the illusion of the phenomenal world, escaping the cycle of death and rebirth and experiencing nirvana, the final extinction of ego and personal desire and an indescribable state of ultimate bliss.

The Buddhist doctrines of sunyata and Anatman are not readily apparent to human experience. Why is this so? The notions of emptiness, no-self and the interconnectedness of all things are so distant from our common experience and understanding because we are in need of enlightenment. For Buddhism, the path to enlightenment, or nirvana, is the discovery, understanding and practice of the Four Noble Truths and the Noble Eightfold Path. The Four Noble Truths are these:

> The existence of suffering (dukha) – life is suffering.
> The arising of suffering (samudaya) – the cause of suffering is attachment and selfish desire.
> The cessation of suffering (nirodha) – the path out of suffering is the cessation of attachment and selfish desire.
> The way of cessation (marga) – the path for achieving the cessation of attachment and selfish desire is the Noble Eightfold Path.

There is a progression here. First is the understanding that in the continuous cycle of life and death, there is suffering; living entails suffering. The reason for this suffering is us – our inappropriate desires and cravings and attachments. But we need not be relegated to this life of suffering forever; there is a way of escape. This way is to follow the Noble Eightfold Path:

> Right views – understanding Buddhist doctrines such as Anatman, inter-dependent arising and the Four Noble Truths.
> Right resolve – resolving to renounce the world and to act with charity toward all
> Right speech – speaking the truth with kindness and respect
> Right conduct – acting according to moral principles
> Right livelihood – living in a way that does no harm to anyone or anything
> Right effort – attempting to live a noble life and to avoid an ignoble life
> Right mindfulness – attending to wholesome thoughts; compassion.
> Right meditation – focused concentration on the Eightfold Path and the unity of all life

The Eightfold Path can be divided into three central elements that must be practiced: acquiring wisdom (1 and 2), acting morally (3, 4 and 5), and engaging in proper meditation (6, 7 and 8). By following the Four Noble Truths and the Eightfold Path, we can eventually reach a state of enlightenment in which we recognize the impermanence of all, the pointlessness of inappropriate desire of the impermanent, including the self, and ultimately reach nirvana, a state of ultimate perfection and highest good – a place where evil and suffering do not dwell.

A question that often arises is how rebirth makes sense within a Buddhist doctrine of no-self. There is considerable debate among Buddhist scholars on this subject, but one common answer is that at the death of consciousness (or the dissolution of the skandhas, which are mental events or bundles[10]), a new consciousness arises, which is rebirth. This new consciousness is not identical to the former, but neither is it completely different from it. There is a causal connection between consciousnesses as they form a part of the same causal continuum. In an attempt to illustrate the coherence of Buddhist no-self and rebirth to the Greek king of northwest India, the Buddhist monk Nagasena offered the following analogy:

> 'Reverend Nagasena,' said the King, 'is it true that nothing transmigrates, and yet there is rebirth?'
> 'Yes, your majesty.'
> 'How can this be? ... Give me an illustration.'
> 'Suppose, your majesty, a man lights one lamp from another – does the one lamp transmigrate to another?'
> 'No, your Reverence.'
> 'So there is rebirth without anything transmigrating!'[11]

So there need not be a substantial self in order for rebirth to occur. Again, the reason for the widespread belief in an individual substantial self is ignorance (avidya). In most Buddhist accounts, in order to move beyond ignorance and to experience enlightenment, one must come to fully understand the Four Noble Truths, including the central truth of the no-self. Buddhists grant that understanding and embracing this teaching is not easy and may require working off the negative effects of karma. It will likely require many rebirths to reach full enlightenment. But it is worth the effort, for contrary to some caricatures of the Buddhist understanding of suffering which sees life as a tragedy of never ending misery, in fact it offers just the opposite. Buddhists see their view of no-self and the renunciation of craving and inappropriate desire as the elimination of suffering, and as leading to an experience of optimism and hopefulness. For what awaits the enlightened ones is the eternal bliss of nirvana.

Objections to karma and rebirth

Belief in the doctrines of karma and rebirth are on the rise in the West. Perhaps one reason for this is that it seems, at first glance, to offer a powerful solution to the problem of evil. Arthur Herman, in his classic work *The Problem of Evil and Indian Thought*, claims that the karma/rebirth explanation is not only superior to Western attempts to solve the problem of evil, but that it provides such a satisfactory answer that Indian thinkers were not terribly interested in pursuing it further:

> Since the rebirth solution is adequate for solving the theological problem of evil, this undoubtedly explains why the problem was never of much concern to the classical Indian, and why theodicy, as a philosophical way of life, was practically unknown to them.[12]

This is, in my estimation, overstating the case as the Indian traditions are rife with theodicy myths. Beyond what the traditions affirm on the subject, we must ask whether karma does provide a satisfactory explanation of evil.

There are a number of objections that have been raised against the doctrines of karma and rebirth. For one, it has been questioned-whether they actually offer a plausible explanation for the inequalities found in this life. According to the karmic law of cause and effect, my present life circumstances are explained by my actions in a previous life, my life circumstances in that life are explained by my life circumstances in a life previous to that one, and so on indefinitely, as depicted in the box below.

There are two problems here. First, the solution presented regarding inequalities is problematic for it seems to never end in resolution. Unless a person is perfect in some future life, there

---

...→a→b→c→d→e→f→g→...

The letters a, b, c, etc., represent the life circumstances of a

particular individual; the arrows represent the causal flow of

circumstances from one's previous life to the next.

---

will always be more bad karma being transported into the future. Hinduism and Buddhism do provide answers for escaping this cycle: enlightenment. So perhaps this is not an unsolvable problem. Another aspect of the problem, though, is that in explaining one's current life conditions, karma refers to actions that were made in this and a previous life. And in explaining the conditions one had in that life, karma refers to actions that were made in a life before that, and so on *ad infinitum*. But how did it all begin? What was the initial wrongdoing that started the karmic process? There is no answer to this question, and so in one sense there is no ultimate solution to the problem of evil.

A reply often given to this objection is that the process has no beginning – it is an eternal one. Is this a reasonable reply? It seems not, and for a number of reasons. For one, the current received view of the universe is that it originated at a finite time in the past, some 13 billion years ago. So it is not eternal, as entailed by the karmic account. It had a beginning. If this is the case, karma too must have had a beginning. So who is responsible for the first evil? Again, no answer is forthcoming (although there are some cosmologists who still maintain that the universe is eternal). Furthermore, does pushing the solution to a problem into the infinite past really provide an ultimate solution? Perhaps we shouldn't seek such a solution. Maybe, in answering the question of why a person suffers, it is sufficient to conclude that his or her actions in this and previous lives are the cause and pushing for an ultimate explanation is unwarranted.

Another problem with the karma/rebirth solution to evil and suffering is that it does not really seem fair that when a person who has lived a long life dies and is reincarnated, she must start all over again as a baby with her maturity, life experiences, wisdom and memories completely gone. This raises a host of difficulties. Perhaps one of the more glaring is that by not remembering the wrongs that I committed in a previous life, how am I to grow morally in this life from those experiences? Would it not be morally advantageous for all of those memories and developments to be kept intact? Is it really fair to lose the moral maturity that I accrued in a past life? The problem is especially acute for the Buddhist since, as we saw, in the Buddhist account there is no continuous substantial self which is reborn from a previous life. But if there is no previously existing substantial self – an individual with dispositions, desires, will, memory and so forth – then in what sense am 'I' receiving rewards or punishments from actions in 'my' previous life?

Another difficulty for the karma/rebirth solution has to do with free will. As noted earlier, an asset of the karma/rebirth solution to the problem of evil is that real moral agency is preserved. In fact, moral agency is central to the solution: the moral choices that we make (self-)determine our future experiences. We are responsible for our own destiny; we are the captains of our fate. Upon further inspection, however, the view seems to run contrary to free moral agency. Consider the example raised in the previous chapter of murderer Ted Bundy. Suppose Bundy is thinking about his life as a murderer and is considering turning over a new leaf by turning himself in to the authorities and receiving the consequences of his actions. But just as he is pondering this possibility, a women strolls by his house and his mad passions for rape and murder begin to burn within him. He now has the choice to continue down the path of destruction or put a stop to all of it. If he decides to attack the woman, and does so, then in the karmic account the woman was not completely innocent after all. She is paying the price for her former evil actions. In that case, Bundy is not truly free to act as he does, for he is simply following mechanistically the effects of karmic justice. He is merely the instrumental means for meting out the justice requisite for this woman's previous sins. If, however, the woman does not deserve such moral recompense, then karmic justice will ensure that she does not receive it. In that case, Bundy will be unable to attack her.

The question that arises is this: where is the moral freedom in this system? If on the one hand Bundy is deterministically carrying out justice, then it seems that he is not truly a free moral agent after all. He is just simply a cog in the karmic justice machine. Furthermore, it is troubling to affirm a moral system in which we understand raped and murdered persons to be themselves morally culpable for such acts of brutality.

On the other hand, suppose Bundy really was free to attack the woman. If the woman was not deserving of such an act (which I take it most of us would believe), this would seem to be a serious violation of the law of karma whereby suffering occurs because of one's previous evil actions. If in attempting to justify such actions, the defender of the karmic system replied that the woman would in a future life receive a reward for such a morally gratuitous act, this does not appear to be consistent with karma. For this would run counter to the central principle of karma in which evil and suffering are the effects of one's previous deeds.

One final difficulty for the karma/rebirth solution has to do with verifiability. It seems that there is no way to verify, or falsify, the doctrine. Back to the Ted Bundy example; if Bundy murders the woman, the murder was the effect of karma. If he decides not to murder the woman, that too was the effect of karma. No matter what happens, the event is taken to be the effect of karma. There is no way to verify it empirically, even though the very processes of which it is constituted – cause (the choices one makes) and effect (the suffering or pleasure one experiences) – are understood empirically. We have an empirical system that cannot be empirically verified. What makes this problem especially trenchant for karma/rebirth is that there is no way to challenge its moral ramifications. As one commentator puts it: 'Human fallibility being what it is, the idea that all suffering is due to a previous wrongful action provides a great temptation to rationalize the status quo with reference to unverifiable claims about one's past wrongs.'[13]

These objections to the karma/rebirth doctrine are significant, especially if it is taken to be a rational account of evil and suffering. But many Indian thinkers reject the very notion of a rational account of such things and maintain that the highest knowledge is ultimately beyond human reason. In that case, perhaps karma and rebirth should not be understood as actual events in which moral calculations are literally preserved from one life to the next, but rather as metaphorical or symbolical stories reflecting deeper truths and realities. Maybe what we have with karma/rebirth is a mythical attempt to probe the unfathomable mysteries of a complex and, from a rational perspective, incomprehensible universe.

Further reading

Bowker, John. *Problems of Suffering in the Religions of the World.*
    Cambridge: Cambridge University Press, 1970. (A rigorous study of
    evil among the great religions in the Eastern and Western traditions.)
Herman, Arthur. *The Problem of Evil in Indian Thought.* Dehli: Motilal
    Banarsidass, 1976. (A classic work on evil, karma and rebirth.)
Kaufman, Whitley R. P. 'Karma, Rebirth, and the Problem of Evil', in
    Andrew Eshleman, ed., *Readings in Philosophy of Religion: East Meets*

West. Oxford: Blackwell, 2008. (Argues that karma is unsuccessful as a theodicy on a rationalistic account and suggests that a mystical interpretation may be a better way to understood it.)

Minor, Robert. 'In Defense of Karma and Rebirth: Evolutionary Karma', in Ronald Neufeldt, ed., *Karma and Rebirth*. Albany: State University of New York Press, 1986. (As the title indicates, a defense of the karma/rebirth solution.)

Reichenbach, Bruce. *The Law of Karma: A Philosophical Study.* Honolulu: University of Hawaii Press, 1990. (An examination of the law of karma by an analytic philosopher.)

Smith, Huston. *The World's Religions: Our Great Wisdom Traditions.* New York: HarperSanFrancisco, 1991. (A contemporary classic on the major world religions; includes reflections on evil and suffering in the various traditions.)

CHAPTER SEVEN

Eternal goods and the triumph over evil

In Chapter 3, we examined theistic attempts at making sense of evil given the existence of God, and these included the role of life after death in developing theodicy. In the previous chapter, we investigated karma and rebirth as being central to Hindu and Buddhist understandings of the self, Ultimate Reality and suffering. There, too, the afterlife (sometimes many afterlives) was of central concern. In this final chapter, we first return to the notion of an afterlife within a theistic framework, noting certain types of evils and goods which are especially significant for theism. We then wrap up the chapter, and the book, by emphasizing the importance of a non-theoretical dimension of the issue: confronting head-on the evils we face in our world.

Horrendous evil and eternal goods

We have already explored several theodicies. They were, to use a term from philosopher Marilyn Adams, global theodicies; that is, they were theodicies that include the assumption that in answering the problem of evil, there must be goods that both theists and non-theists affirm. With some exceptions, as we saw, these goods tend to be finite and secular. Adams argues that a shift must occur from the global to the individual level, particularly when dealing with evils of a certain sort – what she call 'horrendous evils'. Horrendous evils may be either moral evils, such as the Holocaust, or natural evils, such as the Lisbon earthquake of 1755. They are evils which are so destructive within an individual's life that it is no longer a great good to the person. She offers the following as paradigmatic examples of such evils:

> The rape of a woman and axing off her arms, psychophysical torture whose ultimate goal is the disintegration of personality, betrayal of one's deepest loyalties, cannibalizing one's own offspring, child abuse of the sort described by Ivan Karamazov, child pornography, parental incest, slow death by starvation, participation in the Nazi death camps, the explosion of nuclear bombs over populated areas, having to choose between which of one's children shall live and which be executed by terrorists, being the accidental and/or unwitting agent of the disfigurement or death of those one loves best.[1]

When dealing with horrors of this sort, Adams argues, what are needed are not secular, finite goods, but sacred, eternal ones. She maintains that an approach in which a general reason is offered to cover all forms of evil does not provide the kind of help we need. For example, is the following really an acceptable reply to the horror of a parent discovering that her daughter was raped and murdered: 'This was the price God was willing to pay for the world in which we live – one which has the best balance of moral good over evil.' Adams doesn't think so. As a philosopher within a particular religious tradition (she is an Anglican Christian), she believes a more adequate response can be provided involving the coexistence of God and the evils in the world. Instead of focusing on the possible reasons why God might allow evils of this sort, she argues that it is enough to show how God can be good and yet permit their existence. On her account, as we will see, there is good reason to believe that all evils will ultimately be defeated in one's life; that in the future, the eschaton, God will ultimately engulf and defeat all personal horrors.

Before turning to Adams' insights, let's first look to another thinker who also provides provocative fodder for dealing with some of the worst sorts of evil. Simone Weil was a French philosopher, mystic and social and political activist of the early twentieth century. She was an original thinker, a political anarchist and a Christian mystic. T. S. Eliot referred to her as 'a woman of genius … akin to that of the saints'. She had a religious experience in 1938 and thereafter developed a mystical philosophy, combining elements of Platonism with Hindu and Christian imagery. She felt the evils of the world deeply, sometimes weeping at the awareness of the suffering of fellow human beings. But she also maintained that individual suffering need not be pointless. She reflected on *malheur*, commonly translated as 'affliction' in English translations of her writings, as a type of suffering that crushes or degrades a person. For a devoted theist, affliction poses a real problem:

> The great enigma of human life is not suffering but affliction. It is not surprising that the innocent are killed, tortured, driven from their country, made destitute or reduced to slavery, put into concentration camps or prison cells, since they are criminals who perform such actions. It is not surprising either that disease is the cause of long sufferings, which paralyse life and make it into an image of death, since nature is at the mercy of the blind play of mechanical necessities. But it is surprising that God should have given affliction the power to seize the very soul of the innocent and to possess them as sovereign master.[2]

One of the worst forms of evil, notes Weil, occurs when such events lead the victim to feel scorn, disgust or defilement, instead of the criminal.

At first glance, affliction, as described by Weil, is perplexing for one who believes in a loving, compassionate and caring God. But it is here that she attempts to turn the problem on its head. For in affliction, she claims, one can actually be brought closer to God in recognizing one's own powerlessness. In fact, in this kind of suffering we can experience a unique point of contact with God – the most perfect encounter with love possible in this life. Just as Jesus finally experienced the gracious presence of God in his passion, in suffering we can do likewise. In the passion of the cross – horrible torture and crucifixion – Jesus was first constrained to believe he was forsaken by the Father, and then cried out asking why God had forsaken him. But in the end Jesus surrendered fully to the Father, and in the surrendering found deep and divine resources for overcoming his suffering. In suffering, he found the Father. So too for us, she argues. In this surrendering of the will to God in the midst of affliction – a surrendering of selfishness and egocentricity – we can be brought in touch with the selfless and magnanimous creator and there receive a revelation of the beauty of God and the world.

Weil is not claiming that God creates suffering for us or, like a grand egotistical attention seeker, secretly desires that we suffer in order to focus attention on him. To the contrary, 'God created through love and for love,' she says. In affliction, we are at once both at the greatest distance from God but also potentially as close as possible. The choice is ours – whether we receive the invitation of closeness, and so receive the amazing goods offered by God, or reject that invitation and so experience hell on earth. It is up to us.

Using the language of Adams, this touch of God in affliction that Weil describes is not a secular, finite good, but a sacred, eternal one. This brings us back to Adams, then, who maintains that within the theistic traditions, eternal goods of this sort are in fact available. She argues that we must move beyond generic solutions to the problem of evil and look, as Weil has done, to the resources within the particular religious traditions for answers.

> Finally, struggling with the problem of entrenched horrors has driven me to intentionally begin to kick down the dividing wall of hostility that some have erected between philosophical and Biblical theology. Philosophers have tended to exclude appeals to the Bible on the above mentioned epistemological grounds – that it is a piece of revelation whose contents are not generally conceded to be true. Against this, I have maintained that the lack of self-evidence of widespread consensus about truth does not automatically undermine its relevance for exhibiting internal coherence and explanatory power.[3]

Adams insists that God will ensure that every human's life is a great good to him or her, even if they have experienced horrors. In doing so she draws on religious value theory rooted in her own tradition. She believes horrendous evils cannot be offset by mere non-transcendent goods such as sensory pleasures, but they can be offset by other sorts of goods. For one, the possibility of an intimate, loving, eternal relationship with God may well be a good that is infinite and incomparable with any other kind of good. 'If Divine Goodness is infinite,' says Adams, 'if infinite relation to It is thus incommensurately good for created persons, then we have identified a good big enough to defeat horrors in every case.'[4] The eternal presence of God with one would thus engulf all the horrors a person could experience in a lifetime. But she doesn't leave it at that; she thinks God goes even further beyond engulfing horrors to actually defeating them. How so? By integrating the evils one has experienced into one's personal relationship with God. She identifies three possible modes of integration.

First, one can identify with the sufferings of Christ. In the Incarnation, God the Son participated in horrendous evil through his passion and death, and our experiences of pain and suffering can be a way of identifying with the suffering God-man. This is precisely the condition for which many Christian saints and mystics have prayed.

Second, one can experience divine gratitude. In her sixth vision, mystic Julian of Norwich describes a heavenly welcome in which God thanks those who experienced evil during their earthly lives: 'I thank you for your suffering,' says God, 'especially in your youth.'[5] Julian claims that this experience of divine gratitude will be so glorious that it will fill one's soul, and the experience will be far beyond any merit of such suffering.

Third, one can identify temporal suffering with a vision of the inner life of God. Contrary to the thinking of medieval theologians, it could well be that God is passible; that is, God is not a detached observer, an unmoved mover, a great cosmic stare, but rather is deeply moved by evil and incensed by injustice. Perhaps our deepest pain and suffering is in some sense a vision of God's own inner life and experience. If this is so, and if a vision of God or the heart of God is a very great good, then evil and suffering, no matter how horrendous, could be understood to have a good dimension to them. For example, consider God's apparent silence in the Japanese Christians' experience of persecution as described in Endo's novel, *Silence* (referred to in Chapter 4). Near the end of the book, after the priest has undergone terrible persecution, the silence of God is broken through an encounter he has with the risen Christ when he says, 'Lord, I resented your silence.' Christ's reply: 'I was not silent. I suffered beside you.' Alvin Plantinga concurs with this understanding of God's suffering with us:

> As the Christian sees things, God does not stand idly by, coolly observing the suffering of his creatures. He enters into and shares our suffering. He endures the anguish of seeing his son, the second person of the Trinity, consigned to the bitter, cruel and shameful death on the cross. Some theologians claim that God cannot suffer. I believe they are wrong. God's capacity for suffering, I believe, is proportional to his greatness; it exceeds our capacity for suffering in the same measure as his capacity for knowledge exceeds ours. Christ was prepared to endure the agonies of hell itself; and God, the Lord of the universe, was prepared to endure the suffering consequent upon his son's humiliation and death. He was prepared to accept this suffering in order to overcome sin and death, and the evils that afflict our world, and to confer on us a life more glorious than we can imagine.[6]

With these sorts of integrations in play, Adams argues, human beings – even those who have experienced the most horrific evils imaginable – will ultimately experience redemption and be able to find that their lives are in fact filled with meaning and great good. In the Christian account she espouses, the ultimate resolution of evil is rooted in Christ for he, as God incarnate, triumphed over evil in the resurrection and makes resurrection life possible for all human beings. She thus concurs with the Apostle Paul who understood, via the resurrection, that the evils experienced in this life are only 'slight momentary afflictions' as compared to the 'eternal weight of glory beyond all measure' awaiting the consummation of all things (2 Corinthians 4.17-18). Suffering cannot be divorced from the afterlife. Another Christian thinker, Alister McGrath, agrees on this point:

> Suffering is part of a greater whole. It is the link between our present state of lowliness and our future state of glory. Theology allows us to see suffering as a window into the presence of God. We see through it and beyond it, and catch a glimpse of the glory and presence of God which lies through its gateway. It cannot be avoided, but it need not be feared.[7]

Unlike generic theism, then, in this particular religious account, the hope in life immortal is not an ad hoc solution. The idea that God defeated evil and death through Christ is foundational to the tradition itself, and it provides opportunity for future goods that exceed human comprehension. For theists who do not embrace Adams's specifically Christian tradition, at first glance her account may not seem at all credible. However, her shifting of the discussion of theodicy from general to individual goods may still be embraced by theists of other religious traditions. In those cases, the issue would be whether those particular traditions could provide the material requisite for offsetting or defeating horrors. Since the sacred scriptures of the Abrahamic traditions include belief in the afterlife, there is the possibility of the existence of many sorts of eternal goods, including goods that may be far superior to what we experience in the here and now. So in each of these traditions we have at hand possible ways of offsetting or even defeating evil.

But is the notion of an afterlife plausible, or is it a mere pipe dream? Is the notion of life after death even coherent? Is it reasonable to believe in conscious existence after our brains and bodies have ceased functioning? These are the questions we tackle in the next section.

Evil and the afterlife

To begin, there are in fact a number of arguments that have been put forth in defense of the afterlife. One type of argument pertains to a dualist view of the self. Many people in the Abrahamic faiths have been dualists as the Hebrew Bible, the New Testament and the Qur'an all seem to affirm the reality of both body and soul. Even within some Eastern religions, such as certain forms of Hinduism, some conceptions of the self entail a distinction between the individual soul (atman) and the physical matter (prakriti). This is not only the case for religious adherents, but a large number of the major philosophers in the West, including Plato, Aquinas and Descartes, also affirmed some version of dualism. This is important in that most dualists' views of life after death involve a self with continual conscious life after this present one. Since the self does not cease to exist at one's physical death, good and evil and their ramifications are not limited to this present life.

Let's consider some arguments for dualism. One argument begins by recognizing a distinction between physical events and mental events. Suppose you have a thought about your favourite dessert. Does this thought have weight, or shape, or size? This question seems misplaced, for thoughts do not seem to be describable in terms of physics, chemistry and biology. The parts of the brain correlated with your thought of dessert can be described in terms of physics, chemistry and biology. The various parts of the brain do have weight and shape and size. Thus, the argument goes, mental events (thoughts) and parts of brains (matter) are distinct; one is physical and the other is not. So, the argument concludes, this distinction between the mental and the physical is most reasonably explained on the dualist account.

Another argument stems from personal identity. Consider the following scenario. Suppose your automobile is beginning to rust and you take it to an auto body shop for an estimate. The repair person mentions that it will take four weeks for the repair. Now suppose you decide to move forward. When you return a month later, you discover that the repair person has gone beyond merely fixing the rust and actually replaced every single part of the automobile with a new part – fenders, tires, engine, everything! Would this still be the same vehicle you brought in four weeks prior? I think we could reasonably agree that it is not. (If you doubt this, just imagine that the original parts of your automobile were kept and put back together; now there are two automobiles.) In fact, we could argue that even if just one part had been replaced it would not literally be the same automobile; it would be similar, perhaps even indistinguishable from the earlier one, but not identical to it. That's because your automobile is just the material parts that make it up. So, the argument goes, when it comes to strictly physical objects like automobiles, a change of parts (and especially essential parts) entails a change of identity.

But what about human persons? If our 'parts' change, are we still the same person? In one sense, all our 'parts' have changed since all, or at least most all, the cells in the human body are regenerated/replaced roughly every seven years. Nevertheless, we are actually the same person from birth. When I look at a childhood photo, I see myself, not someone else. Many dualists argue that we maintain our identity through change not because our parts are the same (because they are not), but because our essence – what it is to be me – remains constant throughout our lives. Our bodies change, but we are still the same person. Whatever that essence is (some maintain that it is a substantial soul), dualists argue that it cannot be physical, for all our physical parts change, if not at the cellular level then certainly at the quantum level.

There are responses to these arguments, of course, but if dualism is an accurate depiction of the self, then an afterlife is a real possibility. Even if dualism is false (many theists are not dualists), this is not the only way for a theist to conceive of life after death. If a person just is her physical parts, and if God exists, could not God recreate the person utilizing that same arrangement of parts in the future? This seems entirely plausible. In any case, if God exists, whether human persons consist of body and soul or body alone, the possibility of an afterlife seems eminently feasible.

In addition to arguments for dualism, other evidences have been offered for life after death. Here are three briefly sketched.

Near-death experiences. Near-death experiences (NDEs) have allegedly happened to millions of people.[8] They are common patterns of events associated with impending death, including sensations such as fear, serenity, the presence of light, travelling through a tunnel, a heightened spiritual awareness, leaving the body and looking down on it, and meeting other deceased persons or supernatural beings. NDEs are experienced by both religious adherents and non-religious persons. One famous atheist, A. J. Ayer, had such an experience which he describes this way: 'My recent [near-death] experiences have slightly weakened my conviction that my genuine death, which is due fairly soon, will be the end of me, though I continue to hope that it will be.'[9]

Perhaps surprisingly, most people who have had an NDE concluded that there is life after death based on what they saw or felt.[10] No doubt these experiences could be hallucinations or delusions, but the following elements of the experiences lend some support to their being veridical indications of life beyond death: 1) they are widely experienced by persons from diverse backgrounds and belief systems; 2) there are common characteristics to the experiences, as noted above; and 3) the experiences are sometimes quite specific, with information apparently otherwise unavailable to the person (such as locating objects in the room during surgery which were not present while the patient was alive/awake or describing an event in another location which occurred during surgery, etc.). While the evidence for NDEs is certainly not conclusive, such experiences provide some warrant for the belief in conscious awareness beyond the death of the physical body. *The nature of God.* For most theists, God is understood to be infinitely good, loving, wise and just. God is not the kind of being who would create persons with the longings and aspirations for immortality that most of us have (pace A. J. Ayer), and then let those desires go forever unsatisfied. So, the argument goes, we can be confident in an afterlife; God will make sure of it. Not only that, but since God loves all persons with a perfect love, he would not want us to cease existing. Just as we dread the death of a friend and long to be with them again after they are gone, so too God desires to be with us forever. God will ensure our existence beyond the grave.

A moral argument. One of the great philosophers of the modern period was Immanuel Kant (1724–1804). Kant is famous for a number of philosophical insights, including an argument from morality to immortality. He argued that the integrity of the moral law requires that justice ultimately triumph – that the very nature of the moral law necessitates this. But justice does not always triumph in this life, so there must of necessity be an afterlife where justice will be perfectly apportioned. (Incidentally, Kant also believed that this argument could be utilized to support belief in a morally perfect God who ensures the triumph of justice and good over evil).

There are replies to each of these arguments, and there are many other sorts of arguments for life after death, but exploring them here would take us afield from our primary emphasis. Suffice it to say that if life after death is a reasonable possibility, which it certainly seems to be given theism, then there are further goods available beyond what Adams was suggesting when considering problems of evil. What kinds of goods? It's not that, given life after death, the evils which occurred in this life turn out to be good. Evil is evil. But an afterlife does allow for the possibility of vindication for the evils experienced in this life. For example, while goods are no doubt lost in the rape and murder of someone, if there were no afterlife such acts of horror would certainly be worse than if the person continues to exist after death, especially if the person experiences the kind of eternal bliss expressed in the religious traditions. A life spent in a paradise-like eternity with God and friends and never-ending joy, say, would certainly affect how one perceives the evil which occurred in her life prior to death. While that would not take the evil away, it may make it bearable, perhaps even in some cases desired. As Mother Teresa put it, 'In light of heaven, the worst suffering on earth, a life full of the most atrocious tortures on earth, will be seen to be no more serious than one night in an inconvenient hotel.'[11]

Furthermore, there are endless conceivable goods that could arise in an eternal life. The ability to forgive others who harmed one, to love both friends and former foes, to give of oneself to others in charity, to bless others, promote and encourage them, and to experience all this from others entails further goods which an afterlife could make available. Given the prospect of immortality, then, the goods that are possible might well vindicate if not defeat the evils experienced in life before life after death.

Confronting evil

Throughout this chapter and indeed this book we have focused on making sense of evil in our world. As was noted in the first chapter, the practical dimension of evil is important, too. In fact, in bringing the book to a close, it would be tragic if something wasn't mentioned about actually responding to evil. The great French existentialist Albert Camus raised an important issue regarding this point. In *The Plague*, a novel written soon after the end of the Second World War, Camus offers an allegory of sorts for the scenarios in France and other European countries during the German occupation. Focusing on the town of Oran as the setting to represent this broader occupation, he presents it as being isolated from the world due to an outbreak of the bubonic plague (an allegory of Nazi evil). Early on, the citizens are unwilling to see the plague for what it truly is, and shrug it off as just another illness. But as time goes on, some of them, including Dr. Rieux – a central figure in the book – sees the plague for what it is and fights it with all the vim and vigour he can muster. But the question arises in the midst of this battle: if there is a divinity in control of the natural world, when we fight the plague are we actually fighting against God? Rieux muses: 'Since the order of the world is shaped by death, mightn't it be better for God if we refuse to believe in Him and struggle with all our might against death, without raising our eyes toward the heavens where He sits in silence?' (Camus, *Plague*, p. 117).

Camus's message is clear. We won't have intellectual answers for evil, but it will confront us nonetheless. We just need to decide how to respond to it. Whether we believe that God exists or not, we need to act against the evils that befall us and our world rather than merely relying on the grace of God to take care of them. Camus has a point. Whatever one's worldview, evil confronts humanity. Whether God exists or not, and whatever reasons there may be for the evils which exist, we have a moral responsibility to act – to confront them and strive for their elimination. Even the providence of God does not negate human responsibility.

Whatever explanations there may be for evil, it is still evil; pain and suffering are real. Even if we have explanations for why or how they exist, that does not deal with the reality of pain and suffering. As Eleonore Stump wisely counsels, 'It would be obtuse to fail to see that, no matter how successful a theodicy is, it cannot possibly alter the fact of suffering. Whatever justification for suffering theodicy finds, it remains a justification for suffering. To explain suffering is not to explain it away; the suffering remains and the grief over it ought also to remain, no matter how successful the justification.'[12] There is a central place for careful intellectual investigations of the possible reasons for evil, but we must never lose sight of the fact that it is evil we are investigating; it is the pain and suffering of sentient creatures (among other evils) to which we are attending, and to leave it at the level of academic abstraction would itself be an evil. As we saw Grace Jantzen point out in chapter 1, theorizing about evil does not entail dealing with evil.

So where do we go from here? For one, with Weil and Adams, we can carefully attend to the suffering of our fellow living creatures; we can grieve about it. This attention should also involve our thinking through, or rethinking, the evils that exist in our own attitudes and actions. Sometimes rethinking involves internal change, or repentance, and it is this 'continual repentance', says Adams, that is 'the best contribution [anyone] can make toward solving the problem of evil'.[13] This repentance should move us to action, for the world in which we live has much evil that we, like Dr. Rieux, can and should be actively fighting against. The theoretical challenges are worthy of investigation if we are to try to make sense of the world, but there is a time to disengage from theory and engage in practice.

The Enlightenment philosopher and satirist François-Marie Arouet, widely known by his pen name 'Voltaire', didn't have much use for theodicy. He surmised that to focus on theoretical issues when faced with actual evil is to misapprehend our moral obligations. As this book has demonstrated, unlike Voltaire I do believe there is a place for philosophical reflection on the nature and origins of evil and an attempt to make sense of it in the world of which we are a part. But I think Voltaire also has a legitimate point. When confronted with evil, as we are virtually every day of our lives, we should do more than philosophize about it. We must act. It seems appropriate to close this book, then, with some suggestions for confronting evil. While the opportunities are endless, here are some practical steps that could be taken in our attempt to triumph over pain and suffering.

Help needy children by sponsoring a child or volunteering your time to an organization devoted to children. There are many trustworthy and effective organizations dedicated to helping children in need. Whether it be sponsoring a specific child financially or meeting face-to-face with an at-risk student regularly in the community, involvement at this level can make a monumental difference in the life of a young person.

Battle the effects of illness and disease. One of the most staggering atrocities of the last half-century is the AIDS epidemic. Since the first cases were reported in 1981, more than 25 million people have died of AIDS worldwide. There are currently over 30 million people who are living with HIV/AIDS. There is much we can do to battle this and other diseases plaguing our world. Again, giving of time and resources is an obvious and straightforward way to help. We can also donate blood, promote safe nutritional intake and sexual practices, and serve in support and awareness organizations in our local communities.

Donate time by volunteering with an organization which assists the homeless. Globally, the number of homeless people is staggering. There are roughly 3,000,000 homeless in the European Union, and in the United States alone there are currently about 700,000. There are myriad ways to help ease the burden of and give dignity to those who have experienced hardship, including volunteering at a homeless shelter, providing food and supplies to a food pantry and donating clothes and other goods to thrift stores.

Support organizations that strive to provide relief, including food and shelter, for victims of natural disasters. Global communication has opened up the world to many of us. We know almost instantly about natural disasters and catastrophes affecting people continents away. We not only have immediate knowledge of such news events, but we also have access to resources and organizations that are poised to respond. Support could involve giving financially or even providing hands-on effort in a struggling community.

Promote equality in the home, workplace and culture at large. It is a sad state of affairs that domination, discrimination and victimization are substantial kinds of evils in our world. This occurs with respect to race, age, religion, disability, sex and many other factors. There are a number of ways to combat such evils, including becoming more aware of where this may be occurring (in the workplace, for example), becoming more educated about those from whom we are different, and engaging in dialogue and discussion with those who disagree with us.

Work toward building unity and respect among religious traditions. Intrinsic to religion is the power to build up and the power to destroy. In fact, a cursory glance at history shows that religion has the potential of great good and great evil. It is time for those within the religious traditions to lead the way in propounding peace, respect and harmony among those both within and without their respective traditions. For example, encouraging one's church, synagogue, mosque or temple to proactively engage in interreligious dialogue could foster deep respect for one another, even amidst real disagreement on matters of doctrine. Joint efforts to promote social justice and provide for the needy could also be fruitful ways to battle evil and promote human flourishing.

Care for neglected and abused animals. There are countless animals suffering from neglect and cruelty. Consider volunteering at a pet shelter, or perhaps donating resources to a humane society, pet shelter or rescue group. Another possibility is to adopt a pet. Plenty of animals could benefit from a caring and safe home.

Strive to help the environment. There are plenty of ways to do this, including investing in alternative forms of energy, rethinking modes of transportation, conserving energy at home and at work, recycling and creating less waste, volunteering at a local organic farm, and so on. The destruction of our ecology has been a great evil, and we have it within our power to turn the tide on this matter and make our world a much greener, ecologically friendly place. These are just a few ideas for confronting evil in our world. Whatever our religious or non-religious beliefs, ameliorating pain, suffering and other evils and promoting human, animal and ecological flourishing should be part and parcel of the activities of the human race. We should not merely leave it up to God or our fellow human beings to tackle evil. For real triumph to occur, it will require the concerted efforts – both intellectual and practical – of each and every one of us.

Further reading

Adams, Marilyn McCord. 1999. *Horrendous Evils and the Goodness of God*. Ithaca, NY: Cornell University Press. (An advanced philosophical work developing the ideas of horrendous evils noted above.)

Badham, Paul and Badham Linda, eds. 1987. *Death and Immortality in the Religions of the World*. New York: Paragon House. (A collection of works from various religions on the subject of life after death.)

Hick, John. 1994. *Death and Eternal Life*. Louisville, KY: Westminster/ John Knox Press. (A cross-cultural study exploring the mystery of death and immortality as understood in major world religions.)

Lewis, Clive Staples. 1989. *A Grief Observed*. San Francisco, CA: HarperOne. (A personal and moving treatment of the problem of evil.)

Noddings, Nel. 2003. *Caring: A Feminine Approach to Ethics and Moral Education*. 2nd ed. Berkeley, CA: University of California Press. (Examines the meaning of caring and how it functions in an educational context.)

Taliaferro, Charles. 1990. 'Why We Need Immortality,' *Modern Theology* 6(4): 367–79. (A response to Grace Jantzen's contention that survival after death cannot be inferred from the fact that God is loving.)

Walls, Jerry. 1992. *Hell: The Logic of Damnation*. Notre Dame: University of Notre Dame Press. (Walls argues that some traditional views of hell are still defensible and can be believed with intellectual and moral integrity.)

NOTES

Chapter 1

1 Hume, David. 1990. *Dialogues Concerning Natural Religion*. London: Penguin Books, p. 106.
2 Aquinas, Thomas 1947. *Summa Theologica*. Trans. The Fathers of the English Dominican Province. vol. 1. New York: Benziger Bros p. 137.
3 Epicurus, according to Lactantius (c. 240–c. 320 CE) in *De Ira Dei* (*On the Wrath of God*). An online translation of the work by Philip Schaff can be found at http://www.documentacatholicaomnia.eu/03d/0240-0320,_Lactantius,_De_Ira_Dei_%5BSchaff%5D,_EN.pdf, page 409 in the text.
4 Some philosophers have noted that 'metaphysical impossibility' is a richer notion than 'logical impossibility'. Peter van Inwagen goes even further and argues that the phrase 'logical impossibility' is not meaningful. See, for example, van Inwagen, Peter. 2006. *The Problem of Evil*. Oxford: Oxford University Press, pp. 22–3).
5 Swinburne, Richard. 1977. *The Coherence of Theism*. Oxford: Clarendon Press, p. 149.
6 Anselm. 1962. 'Proslogian,' in *St Anselm: Basic Writing*. La Salle, IL: Open Court, chapter 5, pp. 56–7.
7 Plantinga, Alvin. 1977. *God, Freedom, and Evil*. Grand Rapids, MI: Eerdmans, pp. 63–4.
8 Feinberg, John S. 2004. *The Many Faces of Evil: Theological Systems and the Problem of Evil*, revised and expanded edition. Wheaton, IL: Crossway Books, p. 454.
9 Plantinga, Alvin. 1977. *God, Freedom, and Evil*, p. 64.
10 Jantzen, Grace M. 1999. *Becoming Divine: Towards a Feminist Philosophy of Religion*. Indianapolis, IN: Indiana University Press, pp. 261, 262.

Chapter 2

1 See Mackie, John L. 1955. 'Evil and Omnipotence,' *Mind*. [Collected in *The Problem of Evil*, ed. Robert and Marilyn McCord Adams. 1990. Oxford: Oxford University Press, pp. 25–6].

2 Plantinga, Alvin. 1977. *God, Freedom, and Evil*, p. 30.

3 It should be noted that Plantinga includes in his argument the possibility of *transworld depravity* (the thesis that possibly every feasible world with significantly free agents contains moral evil) as a further supposition in order to ensure that it is logically impossible for there to be a possible world in which there is no evil. Thus, regardless of which world God has created, one or more individual persons can be counted on to actualize evil because they are suffering from transworld depravity. This move is consistent with the Christian doctrine of the Fall.

4 In fact, most theists have in fact long affirmed that there are some things which an omnipotent being cannot do. An omnipotent being cannot make logical impossibilities realities, such as creating a square circle or bringing about a being more powerful than itself.

5 Rowe, William. 1979. 'The Problem of Evil and Some Varieties of Atheism,' *American Philosophical Quarterly* 16. [Reprinted in Meister, Chad, 2008. *The Philosophy of Religion Reader*. London: Routledge, pp. 523–35. Citation on p. 534n1].

6 Draper, Paul. 2007. 'Arguments from Evil,' in *Philosophy of Religion: Classic and Contemporary Issues*, eds. Paul Copan and Chad Meister. Oxford: Blackwell, p. 146.

7 Ibid.

8 William Rowe, op. cit., p. 527.

9 William Rowe, "The Problem of Evil and Some Varieties of Atheism," *American Philosophical Quarterly*, 337.

10 Rowe, op. cit., p. 529.

11 See, for example, Wykstra, Stephen J. 1984. 'The Humean Obstacle to Evidential Arguments from Suffering: On Avoiding the Evils of "Appearance",' *International Journal for Philosophy of Religion* 16: 73–93.

12 I owe this insightful analogy to William Alston, 'Some (Temporarily) Final thoughts', in *The Evidential Argument from Evil*, ed. Howard-Snyder, Daniel, pp. 316–17. But the chess match between my son and me actually occurred as described.

13 William Lane Craig (in debate with Michael Tooley). Craig brought this chaos analogy to my attention in private conversation. For a fascinating introduction to the developing field of chaos theory, see Gleick, James. 1998. *Chaos: Making a New Science* (New York: Penguin, 1998).

14 Draper, Paul. 1989. 'Pain and Pleasure: An Evidential Problem for Theists,' *Noûs* 23: 331–50.

Chapter 3

1 Hick, John. 1990. *Philosophy of Religion*. 4th edn. Englewood Cliffs, NJ: Prentice Hall, pp. 45–6.
2 Ibid., p. 45.
3 Paul Draper, online book, http://www.infidels.org/library/modern/paul_draper/evil.html.
4 Dawkins, Richard. 1995. *River Out of Eden: A Darwinian View of Life*. London: Weidenfeld and Nicolson, p. 133.
5 For much of my thinking on the matter I am indebted to Keith Ward, Christopher Southgate and Arthur Peacocke. Note their works in the 'Further readings' section.
6 Ward, Keith. 1982. *Rational Theology and the Creativity of God*. New York: Pilgrim, pp. 201–2.
7 John Wesley (1825) in a sermon entitled, 'The General Deliverance,' in *Sermons on Several Occasions*. Vol. 2. London: J. Kershew, p. 131, as quoted in Southgate, Christopher. 2008. *The Groaning of Creation: God, Evolution, and the Problem of Pain*. London: Westminster John Knox Press, p. 78.
8 Stump, Eleonore. 2010. *Wandering in the Darkness: Narrative and the Problem of Suffering*. Oxford: Clarendon Press, p. 14.

Chapter 4

1 Schellenberg, John. 2004. 'Does Divine Hiddenness Justify Atheism?,' in *Contemporary Debates in Philosophy of Religion*, eds. Michael L. Peterson and Raymond J. VanArragon. Oxford: Blackwell, p. 31.
2 I have conflated two version of the divine hiddenness argument by John Schellenberg in his *Divine Hiddenness and Human Reason* (Cornell University Press, 1993).
3 Stephen Maitzen has argued that the uneven demographics of theism is a phenomenon for which naturalistic explanations seem to be more promising than theistic ones. See his 'Divine Hiddenness and the Demographics of Theism,' in *Religious Studies* 42: 177–91, 2006.
4 Hurston, Zora Neil. 1990. *Their Eyes Were Watching God*. New York: HarperPerrenial, p. 145, as quoted in Schweizer, Bernard. 2011. *Hating God: The Untold Story of Misotheism*. Oxford: Oxford University Press, p. 2. Schweizer makes the case that literature is *the* central genre of expressing animosity toward God.

5 To get a sense of how they may have experienced these horrors, the television play entitled *God on Trial* beautifully captures the emotion and trauma experienced by Jewish prisoners in Auschwitz during World War II.

6 Moser, Paul K. 2006. 'Reorienting Religious Epistemology,' in *For Faith and Clarity: Philosophical Contributions to Christian Theology*, ed. James K. Beilby. Grand Rapids, MI: Baker Books, 2006.

7 Moser, Paul K. 2000. *Why Isn't God More Obvious?* Norcross, GA: RZIM, 2000, p. 6. For a more advanced presentation of Moser's arguments on this subject, see his *The Evidence for God: Religious Knowledge Reexamined* (Cambridge: Cambridge University Press, 2010). For an even more academic presentation, see *The Elusive God: Reorienting Religious Epistemology* (Cambridge: Cambridge University Press, 2008).

8 Pascal, *Pensees*, no. 430.

9 St. Teresa. 1960. *The Light of Teresa of Jesus*, trans. and ed. E. Allison Peers. Garden City, NY: Image Books, p. 249.

10 James, William. 1916. *The Varieties of Religious Experience: A Study in Human Nature*. New York: Longmans, Green. [Originally published in 1902, Lecture III.]

11 From *Islam – Our Choice: Impressions of Eminent Converts to Islam*, Karachi: Ashraf Publications, 1977, as quoted in Peter Donovan, *Interpreting Religious Experience*, p. 18.

12 Radhakrishnan, Sarvepalli. 1959. *Eastern Religions and Western Thought*. Oxford: Oxford University Press, p. 22.

13 C. B. Martin argues that religious experiences don't provide justification for religious beliefs because they cannot be verified like other perceptual experiences. See his *Religious Belief* (Ithaca, NY: Cornell University Press, 1959).

Chapter 5

1. A statement by Ted Bundy, paraphrased and rewritten by Jaffa, Harry V. 1990. *Homosexuality and the National Law*. Claremont Institute of the Study of Statesmanship and Political Philosophy, pp. 3–4.

2. These examples come from ethicist James Rachels in his *The Elements of Moral Philosophy*, 3rd edn. New York: McGraw-Hill, 1999, pp. 23–4.

3. Nietzsche, Friedrich. 1966. *Genealogy of Morals*. Trans. Walter Kaufman. New York: Random House, p. 208.

4. Dawkins, Richard 1989. *The Selfish Gene*. New York: Oxford University Press, 1989, preface to 1976 edn, p. v.

5. Dawkins, Richard. 1995. *River Out of Eden*. New York: Basic Books, p. 133.

6. Ruse, Michael and Wilson, Edward O. 1989. 'The Evolution of Ethics,' in *Philosophy of Biology*, ed. Michael Ruse. New York: Macmillan, p. 316. In Shakespeare's tragedy, when Macbeth is about to kill King Duncan, he has a hallucination of a dagger floating in the air.

7. As quoted in Wright, Robert. 1994. *The Moral Animal*. New York: Pantheon Books, pp. 327–8.

8. Rowe, William. 2003. 'Reflections on the Craig-Flew Debate,' in *Does God Exist? The Craig-Flew Debate*, ed. Stan W. Wallace. Burlington, VT: Ashgate, 2003, p. 66.

9. Dennett, Daniel C. 2006. *Breaking the Spell: Religion as a Natural Phenomenon*. New York: Viking, p. 279.

10. Hitchens, Christopher. 2007. 'An Atheist Responds,' www.washingtonpost.com, 14 July 2007, A17.

11. For more on this, see Copan, Paul. 2008. 'The Moral Argument,' in *Philosophy of Religion: Classic and Contemporary Issues*, eds. Paul Copan and Chad Meister. Oxford: Blackwell, pp. 127–41.

12. Craig, William Lane and Sinnott-Armstrong, Walter. 2004. *God? A Debate between a Christian and an Atheist*. New York: Oxford University Press, p. 33.

13. Ibid., p. 34 (italics in original).

Chapter 6

1 While the East/West distinction is not quite accurate, I am nevertheless utilizing this common nomenclature here to abridge the discussion.

2 For examples, see the University of Virginia Health Science Center, Division of Personality Studies website which can be found at: http://www.healthsystem.virginia.edu/internet/personalitystudies/case_types.cfm.

3 Shankara, *Shankara's Crest-Jewel of Discrimination*, as quoted in Meister, Chad, ed. 2007. *The Philosophy of Religion Reader*. London: Routledge.

4 It is estimated that roughly three-fourths of Hindu intellectuals affirm an Absolutist view of Ultimate Reality. While it has never been very popular among the general population of Hindus, it has been influential in the history of Hindu thought. For more on this see Sharma, Arvind. 1993. 'Hinduism,' in *Our Religions*, ed. Arvind Sharma. San Francisco, CA: HarperSanFrancisco, pp. 14–15.

5 Chandogya Upanisad 6.9.1–4.

6 Shankara. 1947. *The Crest Jewel of Discrimination*. Trans. Swami Prabhavananda. Hollywood, CA: Vedanta Press.

7 Find original source, located on page 265 in Philips, Global Philosophy of Religion.
8 Shankara, op. cit.
9 Abe, Masao. 'Buddhism,' in *Our Religions*, ed. Arvind Sharma. p. 115.
10 On the Mahayana Buddhist view, there are five *skandhas* – mental events or bundles – which constitute what we often call the 'ego'.
11 Recorded in *Questions of King Menander* of the *Pali Canon*, from *Milindapanha*. 1928. Trans. V. Trenckner. London: Royal Asiatic Society, p. 70, as quoted in Runzo, Joseph. 2001. *Global Philosophy of Religion*. Oxford: Oneworld, p. 136.
12 Herman, Arthur. 1976. *The Problem of Evil in Indian Thought*. Dehli: Motilal Banarsidass, p. 288.
13 Kaufman, Whitley R. P. 2008. 'Karma, Rebirth, and the Problem of Evil,' in *Readings in Philosophy of Religion: East Meets West*, ed. Andrew Eshleman. Oxford: Blackwell, p. 289.

Chapter 7

1 Adams, Marilyn McCord. 1990. 'Horrendous Evils and the Goodness of God,' in *The Problem of Evil*, eds. Marilyn McCord Adams and Robert Merrihew Adams. Oxford: Oxford University Press, pp. 211–12.
2 Weil, Simone. 1968. 'The Love of God and Affliction,' in *On Science, Necessity, and the Love of God*. Oxford: Oxford University Press, pp. 171–2.
3 Adams, Marilyn McCord. 1999. *Horrendous Evils and the Goodness of God*. Ithaca, NY: Cornell University Press, p. 207.
4 Adams, *Horrendous Evils*, pp. 82–3.
5 Julian of Norwich. 1998. *Revelations of Divine Love*. New York: Penguin Books, chap. 14, p. 62.
6 Plantinga, Alvin. 1985. 'Self-Profile,' *Alvin Plantinga*, ed. James Tomberlin. Dordrecht: Reidel, p. 36.
7 McGrath, Alister. 1995. *Suffering and God*. Grand Rapids, MI: Zondervan, p. 83.
8 In the recent classic of NDE, *Life After Life: The Investigation of a Phenomenon–Survival of Bodily Death*. San Francisco, CA: HarperOne, 2001, Raymond Moody examines over one hundred case studies of people who experienced 'clinical death' and were subsequently revived. For more research on NDEs as providing evidence for immortality, see Habermas, Gary and J. P. Moreland. 2004. *Beyond Death: Exploring the Evidence for Immortality*. Eugene, OR: Wipf and Stock.

9 For his autobiographical account, see Ayer, A. J. 1988. 'What I Saw When I Was Dead,' *National Review*, 14 Oct.

10 See Habermas and Moreland, op. cit.

11 A quote commonly attributes to Mother Teresa.

12 Stump, Eleonore. 2010. *Wandering in Darkness: Narrative and the Problem of Suffering*. Oxford: Clarendon Press, p. 16.

13 Adams, Marilyn McCord. 1986. 'Redemptive Suffering: A Christian Solution to the Problem of Evil,' in *Rationality, Religious Belief and Moral Commitment*, eds. Robert Audi and William J. Wainwright. Ithaca, NY: Cornell University Press. [Reprinted in *The Problem of Evil: Selected Readings*, ed. Michael L. Peterson. Notre Dame, IN: University of Notre Dame Press, 1992, p. 179.

REFERENCES

Adams, Marilyn McCord. 1986. 'Redemptive Suffering: A Christian Solution to the Problem of Evil,' in *Rationality, Religious Belief and Moral Commitment*, eds. Robert Audi and William J. Wainwright. Ithaca, NY: Cornell University Press. [Reprinted in *The Problem of Evil: Selected Readings*, ed. Michael L. Peterson. Notre Dame, IN: University of Notre Dame Press, 1992.]

— 1999. *Horrendous Evils and the Goodness of God*. Melbourne: Melbourne University Press.

Adams, Marilyn M. and Robert M. Adams, eds. 1990. *The Problem of Evil*. New York: Oxford University Press.

Alston, William P. 1996. 'Some (Temporarily) Final Thoughts on the Evidential Arguments from Evil,' in *The Evidential Argument from Evil*, ed. Daniel Howard-Snyder. Bloomington, IN: Indiana University Press, pp. 311–32.

Ahmud, Isham. 2011. 'The Problem of Evil in Islam and Christianity: Suffering from the Philosophical Perspectives in Medieval Thought,' *International Journal of the Humanities* 6(11): 101–110.

Anselm. 1962. 'Proslogian,' in *St. Anselm: Basic Writing*. La Salle, IL: Open Court.

Aquinas, Thomas. 1947. *Summa Theologica*. Trans. The Fathers of the English Dominican Province. vol. 1. New York: Benziger Bros.

Ayer, A. J. 1988. 'What I Saw When I Was Dead,' *National Review*, Oct 14.

Badham, Paul and Linda Badham, eds. 1987. *Death and Immortality in the Religions of the World*. New York: Paragon House.

Baggett, David and Jerry Walls. 2011. *Good God: The Theistic Foundations of Morality*. Oxford: Oxford University Press.

Blumenthal, David R. 1993. *Facing the Abusing God: A Theology of Protest*. Louisville, KY: Westminster John Knox Press.

Bowker, John. 1970. *Problems of Suffering in the Religions of the World*. Cambridge: Cambridge University Press.

Boyd, Gregory A. 2003. *Is God to Blame? Moving Beyond Pat Answers to the Problem of Evil*. Downers Grove, IL: InterVarsity Press.

Brown, Patterson. 1967. 'God and the Good,' *Religious Studies* 2: 269–76.

Christlieb, Terry. 1992. 'Which Theisms Face an Evidential Problem of Evil?,' *Faith and Philosophy* 9: 45–64.

Copan, Paul. 2008a. 'The Moral Argument,' in *Philosophy of Religion: Classic and Contemporary Issues*, eds. Paul Copan and Chad Meister. Oxford: Blackwell.

— 2008b. 'God, Naturalism, and the Foundations of Morality,' in *The Future of Atheism: Alister McGrath and Daniel Dennett in Dialogue*, ed. Robert Stewart. Minneapolis, MN: Fortress Press.

Craig, William Lane and Walter Sinnott-Armstrong. 2004. *God? A Debate Between a Christian and an Atheist*. New York: Oxford University Press.

Dawkins, Richard. 1989. *The Selfish Gene*. New York: Oxford University Press.

— 1995. *River Out of Eden*. New York: Basic Books.

Dennett, Daniel C. 2006. *Breaking the Spell: Religion as a Natural Phenomenon*. New York: Viking.

Drange, Theodore. 1998. *Nonbelief and Evil: Two Arguments for the Nonexistence of God*. New York: Prometheus Books.

Draper, Paul. 1989. 'Pain and Pleasure: An Evidential Problem for Theists,' *Nous* 23: 331–50.

— 2007. 'Arguments from Evil,' in *Philosophy of Religion: Classic and Contemporary Issues*, eds. Paul Copan and Chad V. Meister. Oxford: Blackwell.

Feinberg, John S. (2004) *The Many Faces of Evil: Theological Systems and the Problem of Evil*. 3rd ed. Wheaton, IL: Crossway.

Flew, Anthony. 1955. 'Divine Omnipotence and Human Freedom,' in *New Essays in Philosophical Theology*, eds. Anthony Flew and Alasdair MacIntyre. New York: Macmillan.

Gleick, James. 1998. *Chaos: Making a New Science*. New York: Penguin, 1998.

Griffin, David Ray. 1976. *God, Power, and Evil: A Process Theodicy*. Philadelphia, PA: Westminster Press.

— 1991. *Evil Revisited: Responses and Reconsiderations*. Albany, NY: State University of New York Press.

Habermas, Gary and J. P. Moreland. 2004. *Beyond Death: Exploring the Evidence for Immortality*. Eugene, OR: Wipf and Stock.

Hasker, William. 2004. *Providence, Evil and the Openness of God*. London: Routledge.

— 2008. *The Triumph of God over Evil: Theodicy for a World of Suffering*. Downers Grove, IL: IVP Academic.

Herman, Arthur. 1976. *The Problem of Evil in Indian Thought*. Delhi: Motilal Banarsidass.

Hick, John. 1977. *Evil and the God of Love*. 2nd ed. New York: HarperCollins.

— 1981. 'An Irenaean Theodicy' and 'Response to Critiques,' in *Encountering Evil: Live Options in Theodicy*, ed. Stephen T. Davis, 1st ed. Edinburgh: T & T Clark, pp. 39–52, 63–68.

— 1994. *Death and Eternal Life*. Louisville, KY: Westminster/John Knox Press.

Hitchens, Christopher. 2007. 'An Atheist Responds,' www.ashingtonpost. com, July 14.

Howard-Snyder, Daniel, ed. 1996. *The Evidential Argument from Evil*. Bloomington, IN: Indiana University Press.

Howard-Snyder, Daniel and Paul K. Moser, eds. 2002. *Divine Hiddenness: New Essays*. Cambridge: Cambridge University Press.

Hume, David. 1990. *Dialogues Concerning Natural Religion*. London: Penguin Books.

James, William. 1916. *The Varieties of Religious Experience: A Study in Human Nature*. New York: Longmans, Green.

Jantzen, Grace M. 1999. *Becoming Divine: Towards a Feminist Philosophy of Religion*. Indianapolis, IN: Indiana University Press.

Jordan, Jeff. 2001. 'Blocking Rowe's New Evidential Argument from Evil,' *Religious Studies* 37: 435–49.

Julian of Norwich. 1988. *Revelations of Divine Love*. New York: Penguin Books.

Kaufman, Whitley R. P. 2008. 'Karma, Rebirth, and the Problem of Evil,' in *Readings in Philosophy of Religion: East Meets West*, ed. Andrew Eshleman. Oxford: Blackwell.

Kreeft, Peter. 1986. *Making Sense Out of Suffering*. Ann Arbor, MI: Servant Books.

Kushner, Harold. *When Bad Things Happen to Good People*. New York: Schocken, 1981.

Kvanvig, Jonathan. 2002. 'Divine Hiddenness: What is the Problem?,' in *Divine Hiddenness: New Essays*, eds. Daniel Howard-Snyder and Paul K. Moser, Cambridge: Cambridge University Press, pp. 24–32.

Lewis, Clive Staples. 1962. *The Problem of Pain*. New York: Macmillan.

— 1989. *A Grief Observed*. San Francisco, CA: HarperOne.

Mackie, John L. 1955. 'Evil and Omnipotence,' *Mind* 64: 200–212.

— 1982. *The Miracle of Theism*. Oxford: Clarendon Press.

Maitzen, Stephen. 2006. 'Divine Hiddenness and the Demographics of Theism,' *Religious Studies* 42: 177–191.

Martin, Charles B. 1959. *Religious Belief*. Ithaca, NY: Cornell University Press.

Martin, Michael. 1990. *Atheism*. Philadelphia, PA: Temple University Press.

McGrath, Alister. 1995. *Suffering and God*. Grand Rapids, MI: Zondervan.

Meister, Chad and Charles Taliaferro, general editors. Forthcoming. *The History of Evil* in six volumes: *Evil in Antiquity* (vol. 1); *Evil in the Middle Ages* (vol. 2); *Evil in the Early Modern Age* (vol. 3); *Evil in the 18th and 19thCenturies* (vol. 4); *Evil in the Early 20th Century* (vol.5); *Evil from the Mid-20th Century to Today* (vol. 6). Durham, UK: Acumen Press.

Minor, Robert. 1986. 'In Defense of Karma and Rebirth: Evolutionary Karma,' in *Karma and Rebirth*, ed. Ronald Neufeldt. Albany, NY: State University of New York Press.

Mitchell, Basil. 1980. *Morality: Religious and Secular*. Oxford: Oxford University Press.

Moody, Raymond. 2001. *Life After Life: The Investigation of a Phenomenon—Survival of Bodily Death*. San Francisco, CA: HarperOne.

Moser, Paul K. 2000. *Why Isn't God More Obvious?* Norcross, GA: RZIM.

— 2006. 'Reorienting Religious Epistemology,' in *For Faith and Clarity: Philosophical Contributions to Christian Theology*, ed. James K. Beilby. Grand Rapids, MI: Baker Books.

— 2008. *The Elusive God: Reorienting Religious Epistemology*. Cambridge: Cambridge University Press.

— 2010. *The Evidence for God: Religious Knowledge Reexamined*. Cambridge: Cambridge University Press.

Nelson, Mark T. 1991. 'Naturalistic Ethics and the Argument from Evil,' *Faith and Philosophy* 8: 368–79.

Nietzsche, Friedrich. 1966. *Genealogy of Morals*. Trans. Walter Kaufman. New York: Random House.

— 1973. *Beyond Good and Evil*. Trans. R. J. Hollingdale. New York: Penguin Books.

Noddings, Nel. 2003. *Caring: A Feminine Approach to Ethics and Moral Education*. 2nd ed. Berkeley, CA: University of California Press.

O'Connor, David. 1998. *God and Inscrutable Evil: In Defense of Theism and Atheism*. Lanham, MD: Rowman & Littlefield.

Peterson, Michael L. 1982. *Evil and the Christian God*. Grand Rapids, MI: Baker Book House.

— 1998. *God and Evil: An Introduction to the Issues*. Boulder, CO: Westview Press.

Peterson, Michael L., ed. 1992. *The Problem of Evil: Selected Readings*. Notre Dame, IN: University of Notre Dame Press.

Plantinga, Alvin. 1977. *God, Freedom, and Evil*. Grand Rapids, MI: Eerdmans.

— 1985. 'Self-Profile,' in *Alvin Plantinga*, ed. James Tomberlin. Dordrecht: Reidel.

Quinn, Philip L. and Charles Taliaferro, eds. 1997. *A Companion to Philosophy of Religion*. Cambridge, MA: Blackwell.

Reichenbach, Bruce R. 1976. 'Natural Evils and Natural Law: A Theodicy for Natural Evils,' *International Philosophical Quarterly* 16: 179–96.

— 1982. *Evil and a Good God*. New York: Fordham University Press.

— 1990. *The Law of Karma: A Philosophical Study*. Honolulu: University of Hawaii Press.

Reitan, Eric. 2000. 'Does the Argument from Evil Assume a Consequentialist Morality?,' *Faith and Philosophy* 17: 306–19.

Roth, John K. 2001. 'A Theodicy of Protest,' in *Encountering Evil: Live Options in Theodicy*, ed. Stephen T. Davis. 2nd ed. Louisville, KY: Westminster John Knox Press, pp. 1–20.

Rowe, William L. 1979. 'The Problem of Evil and Some Varieties of Atheism,' *American Philosophical Quarterly* 16: 335–41.

— 1986. 'The Empirical Argument from Evil,' in *Rationality, Religious Belief, and Moral Commitment*, eds. Robert Audi and William J. Wainwright. Ithaca, NY: Cornell University Press, pp. 227–47.

— 1988. 'Evil and Theodicy,' *Philosophical Topics* 16: 119–32.

— 1995. 'William Alston on the Problem of Evil,' in *The Rationality of Belief and the Plurality of Faith: Essays in Honor of William P. Alston*, ed. Thomas D. Senor, Ithaca, NY: Cornell University Press, pp. 71–93.

— 2001. 'Grounds for Belief Aside, Does Evil Make Atheism More Reasonable than Theism,' in *God and the Problem of Evil*, ed. William Rowe. Malden, MA: Blackwell, pp. 124–37.

Ruse, Michael and Edward O. Wilson. 1989. 'The Evolution of Ethics,' in *Philosophy of Biology*, ed. Michael Ruse. New York: Macmillan.

Russell, Bruce. 1989. 'The Persistent Problem of Evil,' *Faith and Philosophy* 6: 121–39.

Sanders, John. 1998. *The God Who Risks: A Theology of Providence*. Downers Grove, IL: InterVarsity Press.

Schellenberg, John L. 1993. *Divine Hiddenness and Human Reason*. Ithaca, NY: Cornell University Press.

— 2004. 'Does Divine Hiddenness Justify Atheism?,' in *Contemporary Debates in Philosophy of Religion*, eds. Michael L. Peterson and Raymond J. VanArragon. Oxford: Blackwell.

Schweizer, Bernard. 2011. *Hating God: The Untold Story of Misotheism*. Oxford: Oxford University Press.

Sennett, James F. 1993. 'The Inscrutable Evil Defense Against the Inductive Argument from Evil,' *Faith and Philosophy* 10: 220–29.

Shankara. 1947. *The Crest Jewel of Discrimination*. Trans. Swami Prabhavananda. Hollywood, CA: Vedanta Press.

Sinnott-Armstrong, Walter. 2009. *Morality Without God*. Oxford: Oxford University Press.

Smart, J. J. C. and Bernard Williams. 1973. *Utilitarianism: For and Against*. Cambridge: Cambridge University Press.

Smith, Huston. 1991. *The World's Religions: Our Great Wisdom Traditions*. New York: HarperSanFrancisco.

Stump, Eleonore. 1985. 'The Problem of Evil,' *Faith and Philosophy* 2: 392–423.

— 2010. *Wandering in Darkness: Narrative and the Problem of Suffering*. Oxford: Clarendon Press.

Swinburne, Richard. 1977. *The Coherence of Theism*. Oxford: Clarendon Press.

— 1978. 'Natural Evil,' *American Philosophical Quarterly* 15: 295–301.

— 1998. *Providence and the Problem of Evil*. Oxford: Clarendon Press.

Taliaferro, Charles. 1983. 'The Magnitude of Omnipotence,' *International Journal for Philosophy of Religion* 14: 99–106.

— 1990. 'Why We Need Immortality,' *Modern Theology* 6(4): 367–379.

Teresa, Saint. 1960. *The Light of Teresa of Jesus*. Trans. and ed. E. Allison Peers. Garden City, NY: Image Books.

Tooley, Michael. 1980. 'Alvin Plantinga and the Argument from Evil,' *Australasian Journal of Philosophy* 58: 360–76.

Trakakis, Nick. 2003. 'What No Eye Has Seen: The Skeptical Theist Response to Rowe's Evidential Argument from Evil,' *Philo* 6: 263–79.

van Inwagen, Peter. 1988. 'The Place of Chance in a World Sustained by God,' in *Divine and Human Action*, ed. Thomas V. Morris. Ithaca, NY: Cornell University Press, pp. 211–35.

— 2002. 'What is the Problem of the Hiddenness of God,' in *Divine Hiddenness: New Essays*. eds. Daniel Howard-Snyder and Paul K. Moser. Cambridge: Cambridge University Press.

Walls, Jerry. 1992. *Hell: The Logic of Damnation*. Notre Dame: University of Notre Dame Press.

Weil, Simone. 1968. 'The Love of God and Affliction,' in *On Science, Necessity, and the Love of God*. Oxford: Oxford University Press, pp. 171–72.

Wright, Robert. 1994. *The Moral Animal*. New York: Pantheon Books.

Wykstra, Stephen J. 1984. 'The Humean Obstacle to Evidential Arguments from Suffering: On Avoiding the Evils of 'Appearance',' *International Journal for Philosophy of Religion* 16: 73–93.

— 1986. 'Rowe's Noseeum Arguments from Evil,' in *The Evidential Argument from Evil*, ed. Daniel Howard-Snyder. Bloomington, IN: Indiana University Press, pp. 126–50.

INDEX